Acclaim for the S

"I can't tell you all the life change that has occurred at The Village because of what our great God and King has done in the lives of Jeff and Cheryl Scruggs. The ripple effect is still roaring through our people. Adultery has been confessed, restoration sought, and healing attained by so many who heard their words. Their story needs to be heard. It is the gospel in action!"

> —MATT CHANDLER, lead pastor, The Village Church,
> Highland Village, TX

"Every once in a while a story comes along that makes a pastor's heart beat faster. Could it be that marriages that have failed miserably still get healed, survive, and flourish? The answer is a resounding *Yes!* We have seen it happen thanks to Cheryl and Jeff Scruggs. I simply could not recommend them any higher."

> —PETE BRISCOE, senior pastor, Bent Tree Bible Fellowship,
> Carrollton, TX

"Jeff and Cheryl Scruggs's personal journey of discovering God's principles of forgiveness and healing is now being used to transform marriages that seem beyond repair. They have been providentially prepared for this. When you read this story of a dead marriage resurrected, you will find hope that any marriage can be brought back to life."

> —STEVE AND MARY FARRAR, best-selling authors and popular
> couples' counselors and speakers

"What this couple has to say truly will provide hope for marriages in ways that worldly solutions can't begin to offer. Applying God's truth in a unique and powerful way is the core of the Scruggses' prevailing ministry."

> —LINDA PAULK, president and CEO of Sky Ranch Camps, Tyler, Texas

"Have you felt your marriage is beyond hope? Jeff and Cheryl allow the reader to see and experience what this elusive thing called hope looks and feels like in a couple's life. It is their hearts' desire to comfort and encourage others as they have been comforted and encouraged. What a gift!"

—STEVE FISCHER, MS, MA, counselor, pastor, Stonebriar
Community Church, Frisco, Texas

"We have been thrilled to see God using Jeff and Cheryl to reach out to broken and struggling marriages. Their humility and servants' hearts allow others to feel safe, and as a result, they're reaching couples with God's message of hope and reconciliation."

—FRANK AND JUDY WATERER, FamilyLife, Campus Crusade

I DO

How We Found a Second Chance at Our Marriage—
And You Can Too

AGAIN

Cheryl & Jeff Scruggs

WaterBrook
PRESS

I Do Again
Published by WaterBrook Press
12265 Oracle Boulevard, Suite 200
Colorado Springs, Colorado 80920
A division of Random House Inc.

Details in some anecdotes and stories have been changed to protect the identities of the persons involved.

ISBN 978-1-4000-7445-7

Published in the United States by WaterBrook Multnomah, an imprint of The Doubleday Publishing Group, a division of Random House Inc., New York.

WaterBrook and its deer colophon are registered trademarks of Random House Inc.

Library of Congress Cataloging-in-Publication Data
Scruggs, Cheryl.
    I do again : how we found a second chance at our marriage and you can too / by Cheryl and Jeff Scruggs with Rachelle Gardner.—1st ed.
        p. cm.
    ISBN 978-1-4000-7445-7
    1. Remarriage—Religious aspects—Christianity. 2. Marriage—Religious aspects—Christianity. 3. Scruggs, Cheryl. 4. Scruggs, Jeff. I. Scruggs, Jeff. II. Gardner, Rachelle. III. Title.
    BV838.S37 2008
    248.8'44—dc22

                            2008031709

Printed in the United States of America
2008—First Edition

10 9 8 7 6 5 4 3 2 1

With humbleness we dedicate this book to our precious twin daughters, Brittany and Lauren. Thank you for always believing, even in the bleakest of times, for the restoration of our marriage and family. We cannot describe our gratitude for the forgiveness of the hurt we took you through. Thank you for loving Jesus and committing your lives to glorifying him. Your strength has spoken volumes to us and is a blessing beyond words. We love you more than you know.

Love, Mom and Dad

Contents

FOREWORD

A man I know was walking to his car after a golf tournament when he realized the remote trunk opener wouldn't work. Nor the automatic door locks. When he finally got in the car, he saw the fuel gauge reading empty, even though he had filled up less than twenty-four hours before. More frustrating yet, the engine would turn over but then immediately die.

After a tow truck delivered the disabled vehicle to the dealership, a mechanic came out to the man and told him the problem: a bad BCM.

"What's a BCM?"

"The basic control module. It's essentially the car's brain, and once it goes bad everything starts malfunctioning."

This man could have insisted on "fixing" the trunk, the door locks, the gas gauge, and any number of problems—but those were merely the symptoms of an overall malfunction.

How often do we do the same with marriage? We focus on the symptoms:

"We need to improve our communication."

"We need to get better at handling conflict."

"We need to show more appreciation for each other."

"We need to have a more unified plan with the children."

"We need to work harder at keeping the romance alive in our relationship."

We can spend a lifetime focusing on the symptoms, or we can replace the BCM—the basic control module. I believe the BCM for marriage is our spiritual motivation. And spiritual motivation is exactly what gave Jeff and Cheryl Scruggs the courage and desire to put their family back together.

From a biblical perspective, every decision I make, every word I utter, every thought I think, every movement I perform is to flow out of one holy motivation: reverence for God. Second Corinthians 5:9 tells us, "So we make it our goal to please him." Not ourselves, but *him.* In case we miss this revolutionary call, Paul emphasizes it just a few verses later: "Those who live should no longer live for themselves but for him who died for them and was raised again" (5:15).

Jeff Scruggs champions this motivation in the amazing story of his and Cheryl's marriage restoration: "This 'change of heart' doesn't mean the feelings necessarily line up with reconciliation. It doesn't mean both spouses are *in love* and wanting to make it work. It means both spouses have turned their hearts and minds toward God and the desire to follow him, and are willing to let him lead the way."

I am humbled by the Scruggses' willingness to bare their lives before us with such amazing vulnerability. There are some who will judge certain aspects of their story and lives, but out of the dross of their honesty emerges the gold of their testimony. This is an uncommonly powerful story of two people who eventually choose love over selfishness and family over foolishness. It is an immensely inspiring tale of how God can make everything new when we lay our sin, desires, and failures at his feet.

The Scruggses offer godly comfort to any married couple facing the normal, day-to-day challenges of married life, as well as those couples who are facing catastrophic marital challenges, such as an affair or divorce. The message—so true and so powerful—is this: Where there is God, there is hope. Where there is humility, there can be healing. Where there is love, hate stands no chance. And where there is faith, even a broken marriage can be reborn.

—Gary Thomas

*Now to him who is able to do immeasurably
more than all we ask or imagine, according to his
power that is at work within us, to him be glory
in the church and in Christ Jesus throughout all
generations, for ever and ever! Amen.*

—EPHESIANS 3:20–21

*Jesus looked at them and said, "With man this is
impossible, but with God all things are possible."*

—MATTHEW 19:26

*Trust in the LORD with all your heart and lean
not on your own understanding; in all your ways
acknowledge him, and he will make your paths
straight.*

—PROVERBS 3:5–6

A NOTE FROM THE AUTHORS

This is a book about the end of a marriage—about betrayal, disappointment, anger, and wrestling with God. But it's also about how we found a new definition of *happily ever after*.

We've written this book to be as accurate as possible. Some names have been changed, but this is not a work of fiction. This is our story.

There is hope for any marriage. Working with married couples for the last eight years in both mentoring and counseling settings has only strengthened this conviction. Our story is intended to encourage, but it can't take the place of direct assistance. We do offer some excellent resources at the back of this book, so be sure to check those out and put them to good use.

We're well aware that some readers may find certain elements in our story offensive. Our intent is not to offend but to tell the truth, and our story can't convey how *amazing* God is if we can't first be honest about how *human* we truly are. We've spent years studying the Bible and providing biblical marriage counseling, but we are not theologians or pastors. We're simply a committed couple who have chosen to share what God did for two ordinary individuals who hadn't given much thought to spiritual matters. The fact that you're reading this at all is evidence of his provision and his ability to reach anyone willing to listen.

God is redeeming and restoring marriages around the world. May your heart be moved to invite him in, that you may know a renewed and more joyous life. Our prayers are with you.

To him be the glory,
Cheryl and Jeff Scruggs

PROLOGUE

Cheryl
October 1999

D o you, Jeff, take Cheryl to be your wife, to love her, honor her, and cherish her, in sickness and in health, for richer or poorer, for as long as you both shall live?"

I looked into Jeff's eyes and held both of his trembling hands. He looked back at me, but neither of us could see very well for the tears—mine boldly streaming down my cheeks.

"I do." Jeff's voice was low but strong. The words echoed in my mind. *I do. I do.*

The minister repeated the words, this time to me, and it was my turn to say it.

I do.

I meant it with every fiber of my being. I wanted to shout it to everyone within hearing distance, scrawl it on the walls, write it in the sky.

"I do!"

I glanced around me. The tiny chapel nestled in the Colorado mountains was awash with rainbow-hued sunlight streaming through stained-glass windows, as if God was personally pouring down his blessings on our little ceremony. I felt a chill run down my spine.

"What token of your love do you offer?"

Jeff and I watched as our twin daughters, eleven years old and sparkling in off-white dresses with matching shoes and tights, stepped forward to offer the minister our wedding bands. Brand-new rings, simple and elegant, perfect for our brand-new life.

"With this ring, I thee wed." We repeated the words, mindful that we'd said them before but knowing this time it was different. I could barely remember the ceremony seventeen years earlier when I'd first promised to love, honor, and cherish Jeff. I didn't keep my promise. But this time I would. As Jeff's eyes locked on to mine, I knew he was thinking the same thing.

"I now pronounce you husband and wife."

Such simple words: *Now. Husband. Wife.*

So familiar, yet so...unbelievable. How long had I anticipated this moment? Seven years, for sure. Or was it more like eighteen? my entire life?

Jeff and I shared a kiss and then pulled our daughters into the embrace. A family hug. We squeezed each other tightly while our tears flowed, and it was all I could do to keep my knees from buckling.

We stood there, embracing, wiping each other's tears, and laughing together. I smiled at my incredible husband, my heart overflowing with gratitude.

So much gratitude. A whole new life together. It couldn't possibly be real.

We were a family again. Who would have thought? Who in the world could ever have thought this would happen?

ONE

Cheryl
2007

I don't love him anymore."

Amy has barely gotten herself settled on the couch in my office when she blurts out her opening line. She is brunette, petite, and cute, wearing fashionable jeans and just a touch of makeup. She's the picture of a suburban, got-it-all-together mom—every hair in place, her haircut the latest in chic. Only her expression gives her away. She stares at me, defiant. I recognize the anger. Been there, done that.

"Your husband." Who else would she be talking about?

"Actually, I don't know if I ever loved him."

Here we go again, I think, my stomach clenching. How many times have I heard the grief, seen the desperation, felt the rage? How many times has my heart broken for a despairing woman who's come for counseling because she's lost all hope of her marriage ever working? There are so many hurting couples, so many troubled souls.

"Okay. Let's talk about it." I open my notepad and prepare to hear the familiar words. She has no feelings left. She is numb. Wants out of the marriage. Never should have married him in the first place. What was she thinking? Picked the wrong guy.

Amy takes a breath and hardly veers from the speech I'd anticipated. "We're separated right now. John doesn't love me—he doesn't even know me. It feels like he never wanted to know me. We don't talk—we never have. He doesn't care who I am." She pauses. "I know this is wrong. I feel bad about the kids and everything, but I can't take it anymore. I don't feel like I can do this one more day." She looks away. There is more, but she's suddenly clammed up.

"Sounds like you're in a lot of pain."

She fidgets. Her stony glare has departed, and now her eyes flit around the edges of the room. I try again.

"Can you tell me why you don't love him anymore?"

"I told you—he doesn't love me. It's dead. There's nothing *there*. This isn't a *marriage*. I'm done."

"Why did you want to talk to me?"

"I just… I didn't know what to do. I want out. But I know I'm supposed to…you know, try. Everyone says get counseling. So here I am."

"Are you looking for a way out, or are you hoping we might find a way to make your marriage work?"

The defiant stare is back. She looks at me, her eyes steely. "No, I… I can't do it." She is suddenly looking at her lap.

I consider her eyes, her body language. I try to listen to the words she hasn't spoken. She's clearly battered, beaten up emotionally. She feels unloved and worthless. And I wonder, *Has she met someone who makes her feel loved again?*

I've never met Amy before, but I've seen her countless times, sitting here on my office couch…or sobbing to me over coffee. Other Amys. Other women who find themselves at the same terrible crossroads.

I was Amy once. And while my heart breaks for her, it simultaneously surges with hope. If only…

Oh, God… My silent words are a prayer, both for Amy and for me.

Cheryl
1992

August 21, 1992. The worst day of my life.

Ten years after walking down the aisle as a young, hope-filled bride, I walked into a courtroom to claim a different kind of hope: liberation from my awful marriage. This was the day I'd obtain the freedom to be with my new love, the soul mate I thought I'd finally found. Today I'd hold in my hands the piece of paper I'd been coveting, the ticket to a whole new and *much better* life. I stood in front of the judge and told him I wanted a divorce.

Earlier that morning, I lay in bed for a moment after shutting off the alarm, groggy with sleep. *Something's happening today. What is it?* I tried to clear the fog from my brain, and then my heart lurched as I remembered. *Today's the day!*

I waited for the excitement to kick in. *You're free today, Cheryl! You've been waiting for this for so long!* But I felt heavy and unable to move. *What is wrong with me?*

The morning passed in a haze as I readied Brittany and Lauren for preschool and got the three of us out the door. I tried to ignore the dull ache in my stomach. Breakfast was out of the question, and it was all I could do to sip a cup of coffee.

After dropping off the girls, I sat in traffic on my way to the Collin County Courthouse in McKinney, Texas. With a few moments to think, I tried talking some sense into myself. *Buck up, girl! This is what you wanted…the day you've been waiting for! You're finally going to be happy.*

For the tiniest moment, I glimpsed a truth I didn't want to see through a crack in the strong facade I'd built around myself. What if I was making a mistake? What if my traitorous stomach was trying to tell me something? No.

I won't go there. I'm almost to the courthouse; I'm about to get what I wanted. I've always worked so hard, and getting what I want has never come easily. Right now, what I want is freedom, and by gosh, I am going to get it. I can't allow any negative thoughts to distract me.

The cold institutional hallway of the courthouse gave me shivers as I stood waiting for an elevator. Although the hustle and bustle of people surrounded me, I had never felt more alone. But I had on a classy suit, stylish heels, and my best determined smile, and I maintained my composure like a pro. Nobody would know I had the least bit of emotion in me. The reality was that feelings swirled inside my head and my heart, and I just wanted to go home, pull the covers over my head, and pretend my life did not exist.

I met my attorney at the door of the courtroom.

"Good morning." His voice was low and smooth, all business. "Today's the day."

I nodded, uncharacteristically mute.

I don't remember what happened next. I suppose there were other cases before the judge, other lives being turned upside down. All I know for sure is that my internal battle was raging and I fought to keep it quiet, to disregard it altogether, and make sure the cool detached expression remained plastered on my face.

Finally it was my turn, and I stood, trembling visibly, next to my lawyer, facing the judge. Words were spoken; questions were asked. Did I want a divorce? Yes.

But at the moment, I couldn't remember why.

The judge wanted to know why my husband wasn't there. How could I tell him that Jeff had not wanted the divorce? That he'd fought against it? Through tears of anguish he'd pleaded with me to change my mind. He prayed for reconciliation. He hoped for another chance. He yearned for my heart to soften. But he lost.

At that instant, standing in the courtroom, I felt like a horrible person. I wanted to turn to the strangers around me and let them know I was a good person. I really was. I loved being a wife and wanted to be a good one. I absolutely loved being a mom. Yet I could not go on in the emptiness…or in the dreadful lack of intimacy. I was dedicated and loyal, trustworthy and sweet. But I could not see any other way out of the chronic ache I had felt for years. I had worked it out in my mind and saw no option other than to escape and start over. I knew I would have a label now, even in Jeff's mind, of being an adulterer and a mean person. But the truth was that I was broken and hurting. How could I tell everyone this when my actions seemed to say the opposite?

"Jeff needed to work today," I told the judge, who nodded. I don't think he believed it for a second.

Jeff was at the office, all right. I stood in front of the bench, wondering what was running through his mind as he sat at his desk attempting to work. Would he cry? Was he angry? How was he dealing with the fact that his marriage and family were being ripped apart? How did he feel knowing he would soon officially be a single, divorced dad?

And what right had I to be worried about any of that? I was the cause of it. It was a little late for me to be worried about Jeff's feelings.

"Divorce granted." The gavel went down with an authoritative thud. Was it my imagination, or did the judge look a little sad? Perhaps disappointed. I wondered what it must be like to preside over the dissolution of families all day long. That word—*dissolution*—so cold and impersonal. I think the judge knew better. I think he knew he was seeing devastation… wreckage…sorrow…and there was nothing he could do but bang his gavel.

The sound of that gavel nearly did me in. My hand went to my chest as I felt my heart explode into palpitations like I'd never felt before. The urge to throw up became overwhelming, and it took every ounce of willpower to steady myself and walk to the rear of the courtroom.

My echoing footsteps seemed to pound in my head as I walked down the dreary hallway. Next to me, my attorney was oblivious, moving quickly as always, focused on his dinner plans or his next case. He stopped when we reached the front entrance to the courthouse. At the top of the steps, he offered his hand.

"Congratulations," he said, giving me a satisfied, *I-just-won-a-case* smile.

"Mmm hmm…" I shook his hand, but could not muster a response.

"Congratulations." Did I deserve that? Did he? Something told me the answer was no. But this was what I'd wanted, fought for, worked toward. And here it was.

As I drove away from the courthouse, I finally admitted to myself that I was confused. I had honestly expected to feel elated on this day, ready to break out the champagne and celebrate. I hadn't allowed myself to doubt the course I was on. For over two years I had known in my heart that divorce was the right way to go. The *only* way to go. It was the single remedy I could fathom for my despairing hopelessness—the only way to find *happiness*. It was the only way to finally be with my new love, who was even now awaiting my phone call. I scolded myself for being so emotional and decided it was just the newness of the situation that was making me feel so desolate. Soon the excitement of freedom would kick in. Besides, I had no time for wallowing. I had to get to the bank.

I stood in the crowded line, tapping my foot, my eyes darting around impatiently at all the people waiting to do their banking. Was anyone else here to divide up a shared existence? It struck me as odd that a relationship—a life—could be reduced to a few lines on a computer screen and declared finished as the numbers were separated and allocated. One life becomes two, just like that. Visions of my sweet family flashed in my mind—family portraits, candid shots—but I thrust them away, an expert now at doing so.

"How are you today?" the teller asked, as I pushed my paperwork toward her.

"Okay." I managed a bittersweet smile. As she clicked her keyboard and took care of the details of financial distribution, she must have known better. But she gave me a perky smile right back.

"Let me go print out the checks." She walked away as I nodded.

Half an hour later I stood hesitantly at Jeff's office and gave a small knock. He looked up and slowly leaned back in his chair, hands behind his head. His red and swollen eyes spoke volumes. But his face was hard, giving nothing away. If I had to say what I saw in his expression, I would have said disbelief. He truly could not fathom that this was happening.

I inched my way toward his desk and held out the check for his half. I couldn't say anything, and neither could he. Jeff looked at the check, then as he tilted his head, his eyes met mine. His hand did not lift to take the check. Slowly I lowered it to the desk, and Jeff's eyes followed it. He stared at the piece of paper.

I read his mind and answered silently. *Yes, this is what it comes down to. A number with a dollar sign next to it.*

I turned and walked slowly toward the door. When I got there, I stopped and faced him again, my eyes brimming with tears and my heart aching with sorrow. I wanted to run into his arms but held myself back, briefly wondering at this crazy desire. What was wrong with me?

The look on his face stung. I couldn't believe that after all this time he could still appear so…shocked. I had to ask him a question.

"Did you really think this was going to happen?"

I don't know what I expected him to say. Part of me harbored an irrational hope that Jeff would suddenly be happy about the divorce—that he would confirm that I'd done the right thing. I needed to hear it. I needed absolution.

"Not until this very moment, Cheryl."

For a moment I stood paralyzed as the truth hit me. There is not a more heartbreaking sight in the world than a man whose spirit has been crushed. That was the man I saw in front of me. My *ex*-husband.

I quietly opened the door and walked out of Jeff's office, out of his life. *For good,* I thought. My life and my family's lives were changed forever.

Two

Cheryl
Memphis, 1981

C heryl, check out that guy. I think he's staring at you." It was a common-enough whisper between the waitresses at this upscale dinner club. I looked up, and sure enough, standing in the doorway of the restaurant was the most gorgeous guy I'd ever seen. He saw me looking at him, and neither of us looked away.

"He's okay," I shot back in my usual nonchalant way.

"Yeah, right."

"Doesn't matter anyway," I grinned. "I already have a boyfriend."

Of course, Jeff and his friend ended up sitting in my section.

"Hi, my name's Cheryl. Can I get you anything?" I was trying to act normal, but my gaze kept returning to Jeff's face. His eyes sparkled as if he knew a secret. He watched me so intently that I began to feel self-conscious. I felt the sparks flying between us, even though we were surrounded by other people and the noise of the cocktail lounge. I had a great time serving his table, spending more time there than necessary to make sure everything was perfect.

A couple of hours later, Jeff fumbled with his wallet to pay the bill.

"So…would you be interested in going out with me sometime?" His offer was so sweet it made me blush.

"Um…I can't. Sorry."

He was so smooth. My rejection didn't even seem to faze him.

"Okay, then," he said, but his eyes twinkled in amusement.

After that first evening, I saw him regularly at the restaurant. Each time we'd banter and he'd ask me out. I'd say no, and then I'd go home and wonder, *What am I going to do?* Eventually I had to break things off with my boyfriend. I couldn't wait for Jeff to come into the restaurant again. It wasn't long, and I was ready for his question this time. Did I want to go out?

"Sure," I told him, scribbling my number on a scrap of paper and handing it to him. Later that night I lay in bed thinking, *Is he the one?* I didn't even know him, but something about Jeff completely swept me off my feet. He was not only handsome, but incredibly sweet, funny, and charming. Still, I thought I was acting crazy. He was a stranger!

The following morning, I called my mom.

"Mom, you'll never believe this, but…I've met the man I'm going to marry."

"Cheryl, what are you talking about?"

"Seriously, Mom. I've known him for a few weeks now, and we're going out soon. He's amazing—you're going to love him. His name's Jeff…"

I'm sure my mom thought I was nuts, but what could she expect from a twenty-two-year-old daughter? I was about to enter my senior year of college, and I'd been thinking about what my mom had told me all of my life—that when the right one comes along, it will be obvious. "Your heart will *just know*," she always said. I'd never believed her, but now my attitude was changing.

"Mom, don't ask me how I know. I guess you were right all along. I *just know* he's the man for me."

As I think back over my growing-up years, I can't recall contemplating much about what I was looking for in a husband. I think my standards were pretty lame if I ever thought about them at all. My biggest priority was a man who caught my eye, someone whose looks and charisma captured me. Other than that, I hoped to marry someone nice, hopefully ambitious, and fun to be with. Jeff definitely fit those criteria and more.

After a couple of dates, we both assumed we were dating each other exclusively, even though we never discussed it. It was just a given. Our time together was passionate and intense, and we quickly fell in love. Physical intimacy came early in our relationship, and our connection was sealed.

Jeff traveled frequently for his job, so when he was in town, we were never apart. We were always having fun. We loved hanging out with friends and going to dinner. Everything was natural and seemed so carefree. It was all about having a great time, and we were good at that. Pretty soon we were basically living together; I just gradually moved into his place.

There was a rightness about being with Jeff that I'd never felt with anyone before. I was completely infatuated with him and endlessly pondering, *Is he the man for me?* My mind had gone straight to marriage, and I was happy to do whatever it took to be with him. Because of my conservative upbringing, I had a sense that moving in with Jeff was somehow wrong, but I couldn't change the course of things. We just kept moving ahead with the next natural step without thinking much about it.

I was aware that we spent very little time talking about what was deep within our hearts and souls or getting to know each other intimately in a nonsexual way, but I ignored it. I always had a feeling we should somehow be connecting on a deeper level, but I didn't bring it up because being together was so exciting. I didn't want to upset what seemed so right.

August 1982

Soon after I graduated from college and a year into our dating relationship, I started my first job in sales for an office-equipment company. I left for three weeks of training, and when I returned, Jeff picked me up at the airport and whisked me off to one of our favorite romantic Italian restaurants. We held hands across the table while excitedly sharing everything that had happened while I was gone. We'd been apart far too long.

"Cheryl, I've got some good news and some bad news. Which do you want to hear first?"

Now, that's *not* what a girl wants to hear when she's been gone for three weeks.

"Um…bad news, I guess."

"I've been transferred to Los Angeles. I'm going to have to move."

Phew! Could've been worse. I let the thought sink in. *We can work around this,* I reasoned. *There are plenty of flights between Memphis and L.A.* I smiled at him encouragingly.

"So what's the good news?"

Just then our waitress brought over a small, beautifully wrapped box with a big bow. My heart began racing as I realized what was about to happen. With tears filling my eyes, I slowly opened the box. Inside was a delicate antique Tiffany-setting engagement ring. Jeff gazed into my eyes.

"Cheryl, will you marry me?"

I absolutely had no doubt that I wanted to marry him.

"Of course!" I blurted out through my tears. He lovingly placed the ring on my finger, and then moved around the table to put his arms around me so we could revel in our new status. Some of the diners around us had noticed, and they burst into applause. I beamed and so did Jeff. Life was really going to start now.

Because Jeff needed to relocate to L.A. as soon as possible, we planned a quick wedding. By Christmas we were married and living in sunny California. We were on our own, and we didn't know a soul in our new city. But we were newlyweds, so, of course, all we needed was each other. Jeff and I both had incredible jobs, and we concentrated on working hard during the week and playing hard on the weekends. Before I knew it, we were living the quintessential Southern California lifestyle.

A couple of years passed, and Jeff and I moved up in our jobs. It was the eighties, and the money was rolling in. With no children and no other responsibilities, we could afford to play as much as we wanted. Fine dining at Beverly Hills and Santa Monica restaurants, days at the beach, shopping at upscale department stores—these were the trappings that made up our lives. We bought a beautiful ocean-view home and felt like we were living the high life. We were both successful according to our own definition— plenty of money, nice house, cool cars, lots of friends, and just being happy. Our life was proceeding just as we intended.

We spent a couple more years in this way, working and playing. Gradually I began to experience some moments of frustration, which I was quick to push away. But when I stopped to wonder why there were holes in my state of perpetual bliss, it occurred to me that my relationship with Jeff was shallow. Our conversations were about what we were doing or where we were going, never anything deeper. I felt like whole sides of me were hidden from Jeff. I wasn't intentionally keeping my thoughts and feelings secret. We just never seemed to talk in depth about our thoughts and feelings. Heart-to-heart sharing simply wasn't a part of our relationship.

I had no idea what Jeff's life dreams were, and I had always kept mine to myself. I wanted to share them with him but thought he'd think they were far-fetched, so I dreamed by myself. I did not even know how he felt about his job or being in Los Angeles or what his childhood family life was like. I had no idea what kind of music he liked, his favorite foods, what thoughts swirled around in his head. We lived a polite type of life, always trying to guess what the other person wanted or needed or thought.

Actually, my entire life was shallow. I didn't have any deep female friendships, which left me lonely, and I didn't have any substantial sense of purpose for living. My marriage was what I focused on. Prior to marrying Jeff, I'd never given much thought to what kind of husband he would be (he is amazing), or what his character was like (he is awesome), or what his thoughts on God were (he had plenty). He never gave much thought to any of this about me either. So there were entire levels of ourselves on which we hadn't connected.

We were always together, but ironically, I never felt we were truly *together*. I realized I was craving my husband, which was strange because he was always around. I wanted a feeling of deeper connection with him, but I never told him. I thought as time went by, surely he'd start to share his heart with me, right?

Jeff

Barbie and Ken. That's what our friends called us. We were the image of perfection. I had every guy's dream—great job, beautiful wife, nice cars, a vibrant sex life. Things were progressing nicely, and I was oblivious to Cheryl's budding frustration.

To be honest, she never said anything. I saw some clues, like when she was short with me or seemed distracted, and occasionally I'd ask her if there was anything wrong. The answer was always the same: "Nothing. I'm fine." I tried to take her at her word; what else is a guy supposed to do in this situation? I always chalked her distance up to a bad day at work or female ups and downs. It never occurred to me that it could really mean anything.

So I just went along thinking everything was great. I thought our marriage was developing the way marriages do—we were happy; I loved my wife. We're both positive people. We've never been the type to dwell on negatives. I think that's why Cheryl never wanted to fess up when she started to feel that discontent. Why put a damper on the party?

But it's true: we never connected deeply. I didn't even understand what a deep connection would be. That's where I was at the time. I floated on the surface of life, thinking that was normal. I thought I was "relating" to Cheryl. It wasn't like we never talked. It's just that we never talked about anything deep, such as our feelings and hopes and dreams.

In particular, we rarely talked about religion or spiritual things. This was one area in which I carried a little guilt. I grew up in the Baptist church and was baptized when I was around ten years old. I went to Sunday school and youth group and felt like I was pretty connected with God. But in high school, I started living two lives—I had my church friends, and I had my school friends to party with. In college I mostly left church behind. I still knew who God was—I never stopped believing he existed—and I'd even pray sometimes at night when I went to bed. Old habits die hard. I'd pray Santa Claus–type prayers like, *God, it'd be cool if this girl would like me.* I went to church every once in a while—again, habit.

Because I was raised to know God, the fact that I was basically ignoring him weighed on my conscience. And that's where I was when we got married. But the discomfort was never enough to make me simply sit Cheryl down and talk about it. Our only religious conversations were about her Catholic upbringing and my Baptist one—just talking about whether either of us was totally committed to our own church.

We weren't.

So during the time that Cheryl was beginning to feel some shallowness in our marriage, I was clueless. True, I was aware of a missing spiritual dimension to life. But it was easy to ignore it.

Life was great, with the jobs and the money and our Saturday afternoons enjoying the sunshine on the beach. I couldn't imagine it being any better. I wasn't a very deep person, so floating on the surface was okay. Why rock the boat?

Cheryl

I had only the barest recognition of the fact that our marriage and my life were lacking depth and spirituality, but the growing feeling of frustration was real. I decided it must be time for us to have children. That would make the emptiness go away, wouldn't it? We were old enough, we'd been married long enough, and we were financially secure. There was no reason not to move to the next logical step in our perfect life. So we added "work on making a baby" to our to-do lists.

Of course, today as I look back to this time over twenty years ago, the question that seems so obvious is, where was God in this so-called awesome love story? I never gave God much thought. I was aware of his existence—it wasn't that I didn't believe in him. Jeff and I had each grown up in families that attended church regularly. But we never discussed spiritual things. We found a nondenominational church, and we attended a few times a year, mostly out of a sense of obligation. We simply never invited God to be part of our married lives.

Since we never talked about it, I didn't realize how deep Jeff's relationship with God had been in his teenage years or that he'd walked away from that commitment in college. When we met, he obviously didn't have spiritual matters at the top of his priority list. So I didn't know of Jeff's profound awareness that we needed God to be part of our marriage. He kept it well hidden, and we were both so intent on living the good life that we didn't have time for all that "religious stuff."

It didn't help that I kept my own struggles hidden. I covered up my frustration. I've always had a fear of conflict, and even though there was so much I wanted to talk about, I suppressed it. Just stuffed it all inside. I never gave Jeff a chance emotionally. I never allowed him to see the deeper side of me. I might have been discouraged that he never engaged me, but I didn't engage him either.

From my current perspective, I can see that God was working in our lives even though we paid him no attention. He did, after all, bring Jeff and me together in the first place. But I believe that our slow downhill slide, both as individuals and as a couple, started because our lives were indeed so shallow and self-focused, with no time or thought to eternal matters. I had begun to feel the frustration of a certain emptiness, and now I know that I was craving God's presence in my life. But back then I didn't know. So we set to work on what we thought was the answer.

It turned out that having a baby wasn't so easy after all, which was quite a surprise to us, since everything we touched seemed to turn to gold. After months of tests, we ended up going through the in vitro fertilization process, a very grueling and emotionally draining process. It was difficult, but the upside was that it kept my mind occupied and I had less time to ruminate on my unhappiness. My hope that I would get pregnant kept me going most of the time.

Jeff and I sat in a sterile room at the clinic and watched the nurse draw my blood. We had been through the in vitro process and had waited the requisite two weeks. The blood test would tell us if the pregnancy had "taken." After the nurse took the blood sample, we sat in the waiting room and waited…and waited. Finally Jeff and I decided to pass the time by taking a walk around the block. When we returned to the center, our nurse approached with tears streaming down her face. What a scary moment! This could be either the greatest thing...or the worst.

"You're pregnant," she said. "In fact, you're very pregnant!"

Jeff and I looked at each other and burst out crying, hugging each other and hugging the nurse. The joy and astonishment were overpowering, and we clung to each other, sharing an incredible moment of connection.

"Congratulations!" the nurse exclaimed. Finally we calmed down enough to ask some questions.

"But what does 'very pregnant' mean?" Jeff wanted to know.

"It means," she said with a wink, "there are at least two babies in there."

I couldn't believe it. Twins! My dream of having children was coming true—Brittany and Lauren were on the way.

THREE

Jeff
2007

I am meeting with a guy who was referred to me by a friend of a friend of a... You know. This happens all the time since Cheryl and I started mentoring couples and counseling people about their marriages. Sometimes I still can't believe how many people need help. I pray for wisdom today, as always.

We've decided on Starbucks. Appropriately public. Not too intimate. Not too much like...counseling. This is just a casual get-together. Or so he tells himself.

We start with small talk. The weather. Check. Golf. Check. How 'bout those Cowboys? (We are, after all, in Dallas.) Check.

I choose a moment I hope is just right and nudge him in the direction of talking about something real. Why he's here, for instance.

"My wife." Okay, good start. I hope my expression is encouraging him to continue. He keeps his voice low, not wanting all the other coffee drinkers to overhear. "She, uhh...my wife says she's unhappy. She says I never... talk. Really, I mean, we talk all the time. But"—he finally focuses his eyes on me—"I'm worried it might be over. She's talking divorce. She's mad."

"What else?" If I don't say too much, he'll probably keep talking.

"I don't know. I..." The pitch of his voice rises slightly. "I thought we were doing fine. Just going along, living life, you know? We're busy. We

21

both have jobs; we've got the kids. It's kinda crazy, actually. But there's nothing wrong; I mean, we were doing great. I don't get it."

"What exactly did your wife tell you?"

"She said, 'I'm not sure if I love you, and I don't know if I ever have. I don't think you love me either.' I mean, is that crazy or what? Of course I love my wife! I don't even know where this is coming from."

His bewilderment is obvious. The guy's been blindsided. He was clueless, and now he's scrambling to figure it out. To fix it. To make it go away.

I know. I used to be him.

Cheryl
1989

"Cheryl…are you okay?" My mom's voice shook me out of my reverie.

"Of course, Mom." I smiled. "Just daydreaming, I guess. You startled me." I was standing at the kitchen window staring blankly out at the ocean. The early morning cloud cover had been thick, which was normal for June, but it was already starting to burn off. It looked like it would be another beautiful day.

"Sounds like the girls are waking up," my mom said, her voice eager. She never had enough time with our beautiful daughters, now nearly a year old. I knew she wanted to get them out of their cribs so she could hold them and play with them.

"Let's go get them," I agreed with a smile. Mom and I went to the girls' room where we found two gurgling, cooing babies—and Jeff, who characteristically had gotten there before us. He was just lifting Lauren out of her crib when he turned to us with a happy grin.

"Look, here's Mommy and Grandma," he said in his best baby talk, as he handed Lauren over to my mom. I reached for Brittany, and we began the day with diaper changes and breakfast, before loading the girls into their double jogging stroller and heading out for a morning stroll along the beach.

Mom and Jeff chatted while we walked, giving me time to think and reflect, something I seemed to be doing a lot of lately. I looked at my beautiful girls snuggled in their blankets, watched the sea gulls swirling over the ocean, and stole glances at Jeff as he pushed the stroller. Perfect husband of seven years. Perfect daughters. Perfect house and perfect life.

So what was wrong with me? I seemed to experience these brooding moments more frequently. Something was missing, that was for sure. My life was packed with activity—I was obsessed with being the perfect wife and perfect mom. I was always busy making our house a home, playing with the kids, cooking, grocery shopping, going for bike rides or walks with my family. I never sat still, and I always had a smile on my face. But I still felt that emptiness.

For a moment I felt incredibly selfish. I had it all. In fact, people told me that all the time. What more did I want? What did I expect out of life anyway? I wondered why, even though my beautiful baby girls were the best thing that had ever happened to me, I still felt desolate sometimes. Being a mom filled me up and gave me such intense joy. Yet somehow, it never seemed like enough.

Somewhere in the disillusion, I put a label on the bleakness and concluded I was in a problem marriage. I was starved for intimacy—emotional, physical, and spiritual. I yearned to be known, to be fully and deeply understood and loved. I craved deep conversation and sweet affection. The gaping holes in my soul were not being filled.

Yet when I looked at our marriage from what seemed like an objective viewpoint, I couldn't find anything wrong. Jeff and I were always kind and pleasant to one another. We still enjoyed good times together. Arguments were a rarity because there was nothing to argue about. Nobody would understand if I were to voice my discontent, so I reconfirmed my commitment to keeping this to myself. I couldn't tell anyone what I was going through because I didn't even know what it was myself.

The only thing that ever came to mind was that Jeff wasn't tuned in, and I could not figure why. It was rare for me to feel depressed or down—that was part of the problem, since I always tried to be outgoing, fun, happy—but I did question how I could be feeling so desperate. I was constantly trying to downplay my desire and need for a deeper relationship. I was in denial.

I woke each day to the expectation that today would be the day Jeff and I deeply connected. I patiently waited for it to happen but found myself falling into bed each night to hide my face in my pillow and cover it with tears of frustration. The emptiness filled every inch of my being. How could I put it into words? It seemed so hard to describe. Fear kept me from opening up a can of worms. After all, it wasn't just the two of us who would be affected. I walked around in a daze. No one would understand if I tried to explain it. I felt trapped.

I worried about my selfishness. I was not getting what I wanted, and I wasn't happy about it. I quickly realized that selfishness leads to anger. I was looking for someone to blame for my unhappiness. It never occurred to me to look at myself, to look at my own spiritual life, my own lack of purpose. I blamed Jeff. So I seemed to walk around angry with him all the time.

There was only one place in which I always felt lifted up and encouraged, and that was at work. I loved my job, but not because of the work I was doing. Rather, I loved it for all the perks. I felt important and admired in the office. I had earned my way to a prestigious position, and it fed my ego like crazy. I loved the occasional travel and the status that came from calling on a very important account. I loved getting dressed up in flattering clothes and feeling the appreciation from those around me, especially the men. But I hadn't even realized how desperately I was trying to elicit this attention until one afternoon when a co-worker called me into his office.

"Hey, Cheryl," Josh said as he closed the door and gave me a smile. "Sit down."

"What's this about, Josh?" My voice was flirtatious and coy.

Josh cleared his throat and sat down, not behind his desk but right next to me. He leaned in rather close, but we knew each other so well and I had let my boundaries down so often that it didn't even bother me. I thought it was kind of cute, actually.

"Well, Josh, this must be important." His eyes held a certain twinkle, and I could tell he was excited about something.

"Cheryl... I can't help it. I've been waiting for so long to tell you this. I... I'm mesmerized with you. I can't stop thinking about you. I had to tell you. I felt like I was going to explode if I didn't get it out."

I pulled back, stunned. I'd been flirting with one or two of the men in the office, but I always thought it was harmless! What's a little flirting among friends, right? I had no idea I was engendering these feelings in any of the men around me. And yet, on some level I must have known. I purposely tried to get them to admire me, to find me smart and sexy and desirable. How could I not have expected this?

"I think I'm in love with you, Cheryl," Josh continued, "and I have been for a long time."

"Josh," I soothed. "It's okay. Thanks for telling me. But...you know we can't do anything about this, right? I'm married and I have two little girls. This can't go anywhere."

It was easy for me to let Josh down because I didn't have any special feelings for him. My flirting had been so insanely self-centered that it never occurred to me I might be toying with fragile hearts.

It struck me that I must have become awfully hardhearted. My self-centeredness in needing attention from the men around me blinded me to the fact that they were people too. They had feelings. And I was playing with them.

But I couldn't focus on that. My marriage was the problem. Jeff simply did not care about me. If he were a better husband, none of this would be happening.

Right?

Josh continued. "Cheryl, I don't want to do anything to harm your family. But maybe we could get together sometimes. I'd love to see you outside the office."

The notion of an affair frightened me. I had always prided myself in being responsible, loyal, and of good character. I thought of myself as a person of integrity. I was not the type of person anyone would guess would ever engage in that kind of behavior. They all knew me as happily married, a loving mother with high standards. Was I willing to throw all of this out the window and risk tarnishing what I was known for?

At this point I wasn't. So I tried to let Josh down easy, and it turned out he wasn't too surprised at my response. We continued as friends—and the flirting between us continued as strongly as ever.

Still, this was a huge wake-up call. My desire for attention had sent my flirting and inappropriate conversations with men out of control. I began telling myself every day that I had to be more disciplined, just concentrate on my work and go home. But the truth was that I was distancing myself from Jeff. I constantly compared him to the men I met in my job—men who always seemed impressed with me, men whose desire radiated from them. I was bewildered as to why Jeff didn't act like these other guys. I was coming home from work, where I felt like a shining star, to face Jeff, whose disinterest glared in my face. It became torturous.

I was usually home before Jeff, and as it grew closer to the time he was about to walk through the door, I would begin to tense up, ready for the blank stare and his quick hug. The "How was your day?" was so mechanical. He'd head upstairs to change his clothes, and I would brace myself for surface conversation. The awful part was getting my hopes up each day that "today would be different," that he would walk through the door, drop his briefcase, pull me to him, give me a passionate kiss, and say, "Hi, baby, I missed you today." It just never happened.

I began to seethe with a secret anger toward Jeff. I snapped with impatience and moodiness much of the time. The only time I felt truly happy was when I was alone with my girls or when I was at work. Little by little I was divorcing Jeff in my heart.

I made a mental list of everything Jeff did wrong. I was afraid to write it down for fear that he might find it, but I rehearsed it over and over in my head. The list was so long that it was obvious that he was flawed and the distance between us was all his fault. Among the flaws I listed were these:

~ *Unable to meet my emotional needs*

~ *Does not know me / has no idea who I am as a person*

~ *Does not care to know my heart, my interests, or my passions*

~ *Does not care to share his heart with me*

~ *Obsessed with money instead of our relationship*

~ *Is emotionally shallow, unable to connect on a deep level*

~ *Has unrealistic expectations of what he wants in a wife*

~ *Is critical, condescending, and demeaning*

~ *Not interested in making love—just in having sex*

~ *Will not engage in conversation / cares more about activities than connecting*

~ *Does not make me feel wanted, treasured, or admired*

~ *Our relationship is full of silence*

It made me mad that he was not tuned into me and had no idea I was crumbling. Of course, while I could list Jeff's faults in excruciating detail, I never thought to look at my own flaws. None of this could possibly be my fault, could it? My self-examination was not to come until much later.

In my conscious mind, I had never considered divorce. It never seemed an option. But gradually the thought stirred, and I began to wonder if I should consider it. Still I never spoke about it, never voiced my concerns to Jeff. I prided myself on my performance. Nothing would mar the surface image of Cheryl's Perfect Life.

In January of 1990, Jeff's company sponsored a special ninety-fifth-anniversary sales meeting, and spouses were invited. It was to be held at the famous Hotel del Coronado, about a two-hour drive from our home. It was eighteen months after the girls were born, and it was to be our first real getaway *alone* since having children. *Excitement* couldn't begin to describe how I felt about spending time with my husband! I was aware that he had meetings, but I just knew we would have some time *just for us*.

During the year and a half before the trip, I had tried to balance my care of two babies and my husband and the responsibilities of my job after I reluctantly returned to work. That effort—on top of the emotional frustration I'd been feeling—had drained me. I just wanted to relax for once, and I saw this trip as a way to do that. It was perfect timing for Jeff and me to reconnect.

As we drove to San Diego and Coronado Island, I began to feel that same old dull ache in my stomach. The drive was steeped in silence. That empty feeling of something missing reared up stronger than ever. I tried to ignore it and focus on the beautiful weekend ahead of us. But the conversation was minimal and shallow as we made our way south.

The weekend progressed, and it seemed to me that Jeff was more interested in seeing all of his friends than spending time with me. Would he ever notice me? My new Victoria's Secret finds would surely not be ignored, would they? Did he still find me sexy and attractive? Did he care about who I was? I started to plummet and could not shake the feeling that I was at the end of my rope in this relationship. This trip reconfirmed everything I had already feared.

Jeff sensed something was wrong. But I didn't want to ruin his trip and make it awkward with all of his friends. I lovingly mentioned that I wanted to spend a little time with him. He didn't seem to understand; he could see me anytime but didn't get to spend time with these friends very often. So again I pushed it under the rug.

I felt like I was finished. Done. Ready to move on with my life. But I knew I wouldn't do anything about it and things would continue just as they had been.

Not too long after the Coronado trip, I walked along the beach near my home as the cool breeze dried the tears falling on my cheeks. Looking down, I kicked the sand beneath my bare feet, wondering where my desire for my husband had gone. I desperately loved him once. I had a deep longing to love him now, too. Where did the desire go?

My mind overflowed with shocking questions: What would it be like to be out of this marriage? What would it be like to be with someone who understood me, accepted me, and knew me for who I was? What would it be like to live with someone else? Why had I ever loved Jeff anyway? Did I ever love him?

Yet, even though I entertained these thoughts, I still didn't move to a place of seriously considering divorce. My heart knew it was wrong. I constantly reminded myself of the commitment I had made when I walked down the aisle. I believed that when you get married, you stay married. No matter what the challenges, I decided to stay committed. Come hell or high water, as they say. I forced myself to bury it all. Yet as each day passed, the persistent thought of leaving Jeff raised its ugly head more forcefully with a deeper intensity. Why didn't I think to get help? My hopelessness had already taken over. Jeff was who he was, and nothing was going to change him. I was stuck.

Random thoughts of other men rushed through my head. My unhappiness had created a vacuum that begged to be filled. I had booted Jeff out of my heart, and now I was allowing my fantasy life to replace him.

I dreamed about being in another place and time with another man. I had trouble controlling the thoughts, and for some reason I felt an emotional comfort in them. They brought me temporary fulfillment and peace. Still, I knew right from wrong. And these thoughts were wrong.

Gradually, the daydreams became more frequent. At the same time, a feeling that I was dying inside grew stronger. I didn't want to be dying inside.

Sometimes I would stare at my husband across the dinner table and think, *Someone has to be blamed for this mess. So it must be him.* He was the one at fault. After all, marriage was supposed to satisfy all my needs, wasn't it? *I am angry,* I thought.

I hadn't crossed any physical line that others might notice, but I found myself crossing it in my mind. Although I imagined being with another man, my actions continued to fit my picture of a faithful wife. But wasn't daydreaming about unfaithful acts just as bad as actually being unfaithful? I honestly didn't want to be. But the pull was strong. Why was I dealing with this? I knew right from wrong.

March 1990

Brittany and Lauren were twenty months old when I headed to Florida for my company's national sales meeting. My tired body was looking forward to a week of fun away from the everyday stresses of life. The meeting went great, and I enjoyed the friendly camaraderie of folks from all over the country whom I'd known for years.

Toward the end of the week, the company hosted a dinner. It began with a cocktail hour, which I spent on the veranda talking with a few people, including Todd, an acquaintance who worked for our company in northern California. I soon noticed it was just the two of us outside, but our conversation was so enjoyable I didn't feel uncomfortable.

A half hour later I was eating my dinner and sipping a glass of wine when I looked across the table at Todd. Our eyes caught, and his gaze seemed so warm and intimate that I wondered, *Is something going on here?* But he was married; I was married. I told myself that we'd known each other for years, so it was safe—right?

After dinner we talked some more. I can't remember all of our conversation. What sticks in my mind is the way the feelings ricocheted inside me as we spoke and how the banter seemed to flow so easily. I felt myself being pulled in, as if by a magnet, but I ignored the intensity. I chalked it up to many years of friendship.

"What is it about marriage, Cheryl?" he asked, a longing in his voice that sounded so familiar. "You start off thinking this person will *complete* you. And then...there's this distance. I can't explain it."

Todd seemed to echo my thoughts. I leaned in, identifying deeply with his words and eager to tell him I understood. "Exactly. It's like the spark just goes out. I don't know how, when, or why. It's awful."

"I just need someone to understand me...you know what I mean?"

Our eyes locked. I *did* know what he meant, and I knew we were both thinking the same thing. Our conversation lasted a long time. I was oblivious to how much time passed or who was around. I had ignited the connection with this man, and it went beyond any relationship I'd ever had with anyone. Part of me knew the trouble I was in, and something in the back of my brain whispered, "Run!"

But my heart had already crossed the line, and I did not know how to get it back. Later that night, I stretched out on my hotel bed feeling like I had been hit with a baseball bat. Sleeping was out of the question. Why was I so overwhelmed?

The thought of going back to this man's hotel room had floated in and out of my mind throughout the evening. I desired it some; I was curious for sure. Mostly I was desperate for physical closeness and intimacy. But there was absolutely no way I was about to go there. I felt as though I had gone too far already, even in the conversation, and I was heavy with guilt. He posed the option indirectly—just little comments about how sexy he thought I was. I kept getting a vision of Jeff and the girls, like I was having an out of body experience. I felt guilt, yet I was also on the highest high I'd ever experienced emotionally.

I had to shake this thing. Todd had asked me to have breakfast in the morning, and I decided I would not show up. I had my husband and sweet little girls to go home to the next day. I thought about Jeff. I hadn't missed him much and tried to fight the reality of not wanting to go home to him. What did we have to talk about? I missed my little girls, but I had already been unhappy for so long… I didn't miss Jeff.

I showed up for breakfast.

Those minutes spent with Todd were surreal. We talked, but the conversation wasn't important. The feelings flowing between us—between the words—were so powerful it was almost as though we could see them in the air. We definitely couldn't put them into words. How had our lives changed so completely, so suddenly?

The sales meeting came to a close, and we all headed back to our respective cities. I could not wait to escape the hotel and board the plane. I was relieved to be leaving because the temptation I'd faced was more than I had ever experienced. I felt ashamed of my actions, yet I seethed with anger toward Jeff. This situation would never have happened if only he were different. In my eyes, he was to blame for what was happening in my heart.

The plane landed. As I walked up the ramp from the aircraft to the terminal, my palms started to sweat. The thought of looking into Jeff's eyes, let alone hugging him, made me cringe. All three of them stood in the crowd, stretching their necks looking for me as I walked through the doorway. Jeff's eyes caught mine. His smile told me he had missed me tremendously.

But I was numb. The girls ran into my arms, and I hugged them tightly. Jeff put his arms around me. As I laid my head softly on his shoulder I glanced far off in the distance. A tear landed on my cheek. What had I done? How had my heart grown so hard and distant? Jeff didn't have any clue where my heart was.

If you'd seen us right then, you'd have thought we were the cutest little family.

Jeff

When a spouse becomes disconnected and goes so far as to begin a relationship with someone else, there are always signs. But like the vast majority of married people, I was oblivious to them.

Sure, I noticed Cheryl's moodiness and increasing unhappiness. But I attributed it to the in vitro process she'd gone through. We'd been told that we should consider counseling because in vitro often brings up difficult emotional issues for couples. But Cheryl and I had talked about it, and we'd both agreed that we didn't have any problems, that everything was great! We didn't think we needed counseling.

Denial? Yes, that's what it was. I think men are especially prone to simply going along assuming things are great until something explosive hits them and rocks their world. That's where I was. There hadn't been any explosion. Rumblings, maybe, but that's to be expected in life. When it came to her feelings, my wife was an expert at camouflaging them, and I wasn't persistent enough to ferret them out.

I didn't know enough to watch for danger zones in our marriage. That's why I'm so committed to mentoring young couples, especially young men, these days. We didn't have any positive marriage role models walking beside us when we were younger. I didn't have any specific male friend that I could talk to. I had a decent relationship with my dad, but he was clear across the country. I think if we'd known and trusted an older married couple, a couple who could show us when we were getting into trouble, it could have been different.

I know a guy who works out every day at the gym. He's a good-looking, divorced, thirty-five-year-old man with three beautiful kids. Across the gym he sees a beautiful blonde and wonders if she's married. He moseys over to where she is. Turns out she has a ring on her finger. He makes innocent small talk with her, and she responds. It seems harmless. Several months later they both realize they have developed a relationship and secretly look forward to seeing each other while they work out. He is aware it has become more than a casual acquaintance. They have not crossed the line, but he finds himself attracted to her physically and daydreaming about making love to her. She does the same. He has feelings. So does she. He has nothing to lose, except his dignity, since he already lost his family a year earlier for similar behavior. Her family is now in danger.

I see this all the time. People are hurt and lonely and keeping it to themselves. I know this is where Cheryl was, but back then, I really didn't know it. I kept thinking she was dealing with the "normal" stresses of being a working mom. I rationalized her behavior so that I never had to see it as anything serious. But Cheryl was really hurting. In that state, people are so vulnerable. Innocent conversations can quickly turn into full-blown disaster. It was happening right there under my nose with my own wife, and I didn't know it.

FOUR

Cheryl
March 1990

I didn't want to have an affair.

I'd daydreamed about it, but I knew I'd never go that far. It wasn't like me; I wasn't *that* kind of woman. I just wanted to be loved. I wanted my husband to know and accept me, to love me unconditionally, and to care what I was all about.

Yet my heart was captured. I'd been away on the business trip for five days and had barely thought about Jeff. I was relieved to be back with my family, thinking that living so far away from Todd would protect me and that the attraction would fizzle out. But it was Friday afternoon when I arrived home, and all I could think about was getting through the weekend so I could hear Todd's voice again on Monday. Yes, he'd already said he would call me at the office. I wondered how I was going to get through the next three days.

I tried to be stern with myself. *I need to get him out of my head*, I kept thinking. *I need to concentrate on my family. This is where my heart belongs.*

But that weekend I couldn't think straight and could barely function. The hours of talking with Todd had changed everything for me. It was the deepest conversation I'd ever had in my life. But it was with a man I didn't even know. A man who was not my husband.

I'd barely gotten settled at my desk on Monday morning when the phone rang. I took a deep breath and forced my voice to be calm.

"Hello?"

"Hello, yourself."

I couldn't help it—the sound of his voice slammed into me like a hammer to my chest. A stranger, yet so familiar. I could tell he'd been waiting all weekend to talk to me too. That first conversation was awkward, filled with intermittent silences. Neither of us was quite sure what to say, but we didn't want to hang up either. I kept my office door closed and my responses low to make sure we weren't overheard.

A pattern started in which Todd called me regularly at the office. An unbelievable power was overtaking me, and I could not keep my mind from thinking about him. We began to develop a relationship over the phone that felt authentic and real. My heart kept telling me I had never known this kind of soul connection before, and I was quickly convinced that this is what a *soul mate* was.

My phone calls with Todd became almost an addiction. At home, I was on autopilot. I lived for the weekdays when I'd arrive in my office and hear the phone ring. I began to replace Jeff with this guy and admitted to myself that I might be falling in love. I went deeper into thinking I didn't love Jeff anymore and probably never had. The thought kept coming to my mind: *I married the wrong person.* The logical question was, now what? My mind began to create a new life—a life without Jeff.

It's hard to explain how a "good person" like me could rationalize all of this. I knew that every time I answered that phone, every time I took part in this conversation, I was making a choice. I knew that every time I allowed myself to fantasize about this man, I was making a choice. Yet I also felt incapable of making any other choice. The pull was just too strong.

So I didn't resist the alluring thoughts and feelings. In fact, I wanted more. An intricate painting filtered through my head and landed in my heart, a portrait of an intimate love worthy of the best romance novel— passionate and overpowering. Sexual and emotional energy consumed me. It was more than I had felt in years.

Naturally I hid this dark secret from Jeff. We hadn't spoken about deep, important matters before, so we weren't going to start now. I felt almost as if I were drowning, because I could not seem to control the intense, overwhelming obsession of the new emotional connection.

Part of me wanted to tell Jeff how I was feeling. Somehow I thought if I got it on the table, we could work at turning things around, but I was afraid. I was afraid of being exposed and transparent because I had never been before, and I feared Jeff would not like me for who I was. Ironically, I thought he might leave me.

No one would have ever known that our marriage was going downhill rapidly. We rarely argued, because we were both afraid of conflict. Communication between us was about the surface things of life. The relationship was shallow, yet to the outside world, our marriage was what everyone desired.

And although I felt like I was under water, I was, conversely, on the highest high I had ever known. The longings of my soul were finally being filled. The emptiness dissipated. I was *happy*, experiencing that amorphous exhilaration I'd been wanting for so long. I felt like two different people living two different lives. At home I was the dutiful—if distant—wife, although I was moody and finding it harder to maintain my smile. I was the devoted mommy, a role I cherished. I never allowed myself to think that the other side of me, the one that was getting deeper into something I couldn't control, could be a threat to my precious children.

The intensity of this new relationship strengthened through conversation alone. As I recognized how far gone I was, I felt tremendous guilt, but it wasn't enough to pull me out. I could not change direction and veer away from it. The new connection was filling so many needs and making me feel so fantastic on a daily basis that there was never enough motivation to give it up. I felt like a starving woman being asked to say no to a sumptuous plate of food placed in front of her. How could I possibly do that?

I was being told I was beautiful. I was admired for being smart. My sense of humor was appreciated, and my thoughts were seen as important. I was talking with someone who seemed to care deeply about every aspect of *who I was*—what I felt, what I thought, what I wanted out of life. It was a drug that produced a euphoria I didn't know was possible.

The daily routine at our home plugged along without apparent change. No one knew of my intense turmoil. I wondered how Jeff could fail to recognize it, and part of me wished he would.

One afternoon I came home from work, walked through the door, dropped my purse and briefcase on the table, and fell into my chair. I thought about the day. I'd had a hard time concentrating in the office, which was becoming normal. I spent so much time on the phone with my new friend that half my work got left behind on my desk. I looked down at my left hand and stared at my wedding ring. What had I gotten myself into?

I slowly climbed the stairs to change clothes. The girls were napping. I looked in the mirror to see who I was becoming, and I had a hard time recognizing myself. Who is the person behaving in this strange way? I again looked at my left hand. What was I going to do? I knew something would have to give...and soon.

I started dinner and watched my kids and my husband as they played on the family-room floor. *What am I doing?* I thought for the millionth time. Am I jeopardizing all this—the perfect family, the so-called perfect life?

Jeff
April 1990

My world exploded on an ordinary Sunday afternoon as I was getting ready to play golf with one of my buddies.

Spring was beautiful in California—perfect sunny days, not too hot. Everywhere I looked, life seemed great. The ocean view from our windows; the twins playing on the floor with their toys; my wife, who was fun and funny and successful in her own right; my job that fed my competitive side and supported our family very nicely. I woke up most days with a deeply contented feeling. *This is the life*, I'd say to myself.

It was a month after Cheryl's business trip, and I was getting my golf stuff together. Cheryl was upstairs on the phone with her mother, and I could hear the low tones of her voice through the closed door. As I went up to tell her I was leaving, it was quiet. I opened the door and found her on our bed. Her face was in the pillow, but as I moved across the room, I realized she was crying. I paused, taken aback, then went to her.

"What's wrong, hon?"

She sat up, wiping her eyes and trying to keep her face away from me. I tried again. "Hey, hey, it's okay. What is it? What's going on?"

I put my arms around her, and she kept her back to me, shuddering with sobs, not speaking. The moment seemed interminable as I waited. A ribbon of dread began to snake through my gut. This wasn't right. It wasn't the Cheryl I knew.

"I can't do it anymore, Jeff," she whispered, still not looking at me. "I don't think I love you."

Her admission hit me between the eyes, and I was stunned into silence. But there was more.

Tears streaming down her face, Cheryl went on, "I just… I'm just not sure I ever loved you."

How does a guy respond to something like that? At first I couldn't grasp what she was saying. *What? You don't love me?* It was like I was suddenly thrust into an alternate universe where nothing made sense. We had a fantastic marriage and an unbelievably fortunate life. We loved each other, or so I had always assumed. My buddies would frequently comment on how Cheryl and I had it all together. This couldn't be happening. I tried to put my arms around her, but she resisted.

"Cheryl, wait a minute… Slow down. Let's talk."

"No, Jeff. No. I can't."

"But what's this all about? How long have you felt this way?"

Cheryl's tears continued to fall, but she seemed closed off. Like she'd retreated. "Cheryl, come on, talk to me. Is it me? Is it something I did? Listen, we can work on this. I'll do anything…anything to make this right. Tell me what you need."

But she had nothing more to say.

Shock. That's the best word I can think of to describe my state of mind right then. My wife was basically telling me that my whole life was a lie. Everything I'd thought was true was now in question.

What have I been doing wrong? Why does she think she doesn't love me? And how could this have been happening without me knowing? All of it defied logic.

I wondered if I'd been that clueless. Had she been trying to make it clear to me somehow? But other than some emotional ups and downs—which seemed within the realm of normal—I couldn't think of anything. She seemed to have turned into someone I didn't know or maybe—could it be?—had never known. The rug was pulled out from under me. Everything I thought I had built was crashing in around me.

Either I was about the dumbest guy alive, or Cheryl was frighteningly good at hiding the truth about herself.

Cheryl

Sad to say, I was *that* good at hiding. And even after I told Jeff I didn't love him, I was still hiding the biggest secret—the latest reason for my dissatisfaction with our marriage. It was a piece of the puzzle that Jeff wouldn't learn about for years.

The depth of Jeff's disbelief and devastation wasn't a surprise to me. I'd been keeping my growing discontent to myself, and I'd been careful not to leave any clues about my new long-distance relationship. But I was so wrapped up in my own feelings that I was numb to Jeff's. His obvious despair didn't affect me. I felt like I was drowning in this marriage, and I just wanted out.

The following days and weeks were strange. Jeff and I coexisted while continuing to be good parents and work at our jobs. We didn't talk much. I'd look up and catch Jeff staring at me, like he was trying to figure out who I was. I'd look away.

Every now and then, he'd try to get me to talk, but I couldn't seem to say anything. The secret locked up inside rendered me mute. I was at war with myself. I didn't know what I wanted, except that I didn't want to end the new relationship, but neither could I imagine actually leaving Jeff. The dissonance was suffocating—both the inconsistency in my warring inner feelings and the dichotomy between my inner self and the outer one I presented to the world. It took so much energy to keep it all inside that I was exhausted all the time.

Jeff suggested we go to counseling, and at first I blew off the idea. I didn't want to talk about anything, and I was convinced nothing would change our situation. I wasn't ready to come clean with the whole truth about what was going on—I couldn't bear to hurt Jeff that way—and without the truth, I knew counseling wouldn't help us. But Jeff persisted, nearly begging me, so finally I agreed.

Once we'd made the appointment, part of me started to hope that somehow the counseling would make this all go away. I imagined getting some new insight that would miraculously make it easy for me to break off the affair and turn back to Jeff. At the same time, I thought maybe in counseling we'd discover that we truly weren't meant to be together. I desired validation that my marriage was wrong from the start and that I was never in love with Jeff from the very beginning. In my imagination, Jeff would realize that our marriage wasn't working after all—maybe admit he didn't love me either—and we'd mutually decide to separate, leaving me free to pursue my new romance. All of these thoughts ricocheted around my bewildered mind.

Jeff

We sat in the counselor's office and got through the obligatory introductions. We'd chosen a female counselor because I wanted Cheryl to feel comfortable. Cheryl was so stiff and reserved, I wondered who she was and where my wife had gone. I told the counselor bluntly that the reason we were there was because Cheryl, out of the blue, had announced she didn't love me anymore. The counselor looked at her.

"This is what happened?"

She nodded.

"And you still feel this way?" the counselor asked.

Cheryl glanced up at me, then looked back at her lap. "Yes," she murmured.

The counselor looked at me. "Prior to her telling you this, did you have any idea there was a problem?"

"No," I told her. I felt sheepish. What kind of denial had I been in? But the counselor had a different perspective.

"That's not uncommon," she said. "When one partner is going through emotional changes, the other is often completely unaware." She turned to Cheryl. "How long has this been going on?"

"I think…at least a few months. But…it might have started before we even had the girls. So, years I guess."

Years? My mind was reeling. Cheryl has not loved me for years?

The rest of that first session passed pretty quickly as the counselor asked more questions about our marriage. If it hadn't been so serious, it could've been comical—as if Cheryl and I were describing two completely different couples.

"We never talk." We talk all the time.

"We have no intimacy." We're so close that all my friends are envious of us.

"He doesn't seem to care about me." I spend all my time thinking of ways to make her happy.

"He doesn't seem to find me sexy or attractive." We have a great sex life, and I've always been attracted to her.

The scariest part about all of this was how Cheryl's face seemed so hard. There was no warmth. Her entire body language was stiff and unyielding, and her answers were brief and curt. The session ended with me feeling worse than before, if that were possible.

The next week, we went a second time, and it progressed in much the same manner. Me eager to get this all worked out, get my wife back, and get my life back. Cheryl distant, aloof, unbending.

That was the end of that. It was clear to both of us the counseling wasn't helping. Some time later, after we had moved from California, we saw another counselor, this time a man. Again, we had two sessions. Again, they were unproductive. So I arranged to see the counselor alone.

I arrived in the office and sat down, and the session started with a brief rehashing of the previous two sessions. Then the counselor laid it on the line.

"Jeff, I have to be honest with you. I think you're wasting your money. You're wasting your time, and you're wasting my time."

I couldn't even respond. Aren't therapists supposed to help with this stuff? How can he sit there and take away even my last shred of optimism? Later I would realize that things may have gone differently if we'd been seeing a Christian or biblical counselor, but our only experience at that point was with secular therapists.

He looked at my shell-shocked face. "I'm sorry, Jeff. Her heart just isn't in it. I can't do anything to change that. You've seen how she is when she's in here—she'd rather be anywhere else. She's not trying. I don't see any hope that counseling is going to help right now. Something will have to change. It won't do any good unless her attitude improves."

"This is unbelievable," I said, stating the obvious. "How could she change so completely?"

"Well, there's one possibility." The counselor looked at me pointedly and paused. I didn't know what he was getting at. "Could there be someone else?"

"Someone... Oh, gee. No, I don't think so. I mean, how could that be? She would never do that... And when would she have *time* to do that? She goes to work and comes home; she's always with the kids..." The thought boggled my mind.

"Have you asked her?"

"No, of course not. It's never even occurred to me."

"I think you should ask her."

I couldn't believe the counselor actually thought it might be a possibility. But I honestly would have done anything to get to the bottom of his question. So later that week, I did ask Cheryl. She assured me there was no one else—that wasn't the problem. She just wasn't happy in our marriage. We weren't right together.

Cheryl's coldness toward me was a blow to my ego. Yet I believed her when she said there was no one else. I'd always had a lot of pride in who I was and how great we were together.

I couldn't imagine she'd actually prefer someone else over me.

Cheryl

To me, our counseling sessions—with both counselors—seemed unfair. The counselors seemed to be siding with Jeff, and it made me angry. They made me feel as though I was crazy. I was not crazy, but my actions were very irrational. I didn't admit it, but I was living only for myself and my selfish desires. That in itself will make you behave in irrational ways. My marriage was over in my mind and heart. I just wanted *out* and had come up with every possible excuse to leave.

But as unlikely as it sounds, life went on. We'd go to work, take care of the girls, make small talk.

"How was your day?"

"Fine, yours?"

"Good. Want to go to dinner?"

"Sure."

I always felt like I was about to bust. Why couldn't I open up to my husband? *We must not be soul mates. I've got to be with my soul mate.*

I was under a dark, thick cloud and could not escape. It was closing in on me. I was suffocating, and I wanted to be free. I felt smothered by Jeff, even though he was not smothering me. I wanted out. Yet I couldn't make myself think the word *divorce*. So things stayed status quo.

Then, out of nowhere, a breath of fresh air. A blessing, I thought. Jeff came home from work one day and sprung the news that his company was moving us to Dallas. It dawned on me that this could be my escape from the tortuous double life I'd created. A fresh start! Everything had happened so fast…in March, the affair had begun. In April I'd told Jeff I didn't love him, and now, just a couple of weeks later, we were planning a transfer to Texas. This could be the answer to all my problems.

Relief filled me. I would be miles away from this situation; we'd be building a new life and finding new friends—it was just what we needed. I was excited about the move. This whole affair was going to go away, and the best part was that I'd never have to tell Jeff. I concentrated on that bright thought while taking care of the details of putting our house on the market and preparing for the relocation.

We looked at properties in Dallas, and Jeff came up with the idea of building a house. It would be our dream home, large and beautiful, right on a golf course. I was the golfer in the family—Jeff had only started golfing because I loved it—and he was excited to give me the gift of a home right on the links. I latched on to that plan. Another reason for hope. Perhaps this would be the answer to getting our lives back on track. We were to move in four months, and the time passed quickly with everything there was to do. My long-distance relationship was still going, yet in the back of my mind, I expected it would be over soon with our move.

Jeff sensed my renewed enthusiasm, and I could tell he was relieved. He thought I was coming around. He assumed I must have been going through a phase but things were going to be okay. I did everything I could to help him think this way. I truly wanted to believe our relationship would turn around.

Nevertheless, I saw Todd one time in California. We met briefly in a hotel, and it was then that we crossed the line physically, making this a full-fledged affair. Strangely, I didn't enjoy the physical experience (and I'm not just saying that for Jeff's sake). What made the relationship passionate for me was the emotional connection. How ironic that I compromised my integrity and betrayed Jeff for something that wasn't even satisfying.

We moved to Dallas in August of 1990, when the girls were two years old, and rented a small two-bedroom apartment while our house was being built. As I went about the business of settling the family into our apartment, I realized the feelings of contentment I'd expected to materialize with the move had failed to appear. And without missing a beat, I continued the relationship with Todd. It had never been about location anyway. It was a deeply emotional affair. So not only did it continue after our move, it intensified.

For whatever reason, I was able to share everything with this guy. Things I could not seem to talk about with Jeff, I easily discussed with him. Todd had taken the soul mate position in my life, and Jeff was booted out. As I've pondered this situation, it makes sense. It's easier to share with a stranger you don't live with, who doesn't know your weaknesses and quirks and who doesn't see you at your worst. There is safety. Home is where the truth is. Home is where your guard is down. Home is where the real you is displayed. The stranger always wins because there is less risk. The stranger always looks better.

I even found myself comparing this new guy with my husband. But when you're married and have twin toddlers, life is kind of hectic. Diapers and grocery shopping and laundry are the topics of the day. Romance is pretty far down on the list. So there's no comparison—a romance-filled life with a stranger looks so much better.

I entered a phase where I cried a lot, and I didn't even try to hide it from Jeff. He'd come home and find me crying, and he'd assume the stress of taking care of the twins, living in a tiny apartment, and dealing with a new city was getting to me. Going into superdad mode, he'd take the girls outside to play and give me a break. He was so kind to me that it broke my heart over and over again.

But I didn't need a break from the kids; that wasn't the problem. I was simply devastated that I was still not happy, that I was still living a double life. I started to think about seeing Todd. I wanted to be with him. I wanted a new life with him.

So for the first time, I started thinking seriously about divorce.

FIVE

Jeff
2007

Nancy and Dave sit on opposite ends of the sofa, keeping their distance from each other, yet trying not to be obvious about it. They're still polite, despite the problems. This is the second time Cheryl and I have met with them, hoping to help them sort through their issues.

Nancy is a beautiful woman, mid-thirties, her figure slightly rounded, her demeanor soft and sweet. Her eyes fill with tears, and she avoids looking at her husband.

"I need to know if I'm seeing things correctly," she begins, throwing an apologetic glance toward Dave. "Our kids are still young, and they take up a lot of my time and energy. But he seems to be acting like a single man. He goes out with the guys whenever he wants. He stays out till all hours. He plays poker or…well, I'm not always sure what he does. I feel like the kids and I have been put on the back burner."

Dave is shaking his head. Nancy stops and looks up at him.

"What?" she asks him, a touch of shrill in her voice.

"I don't go out all that much," he says. "And you always tell me it's okay."

"That's just it," Nancy says. "I don't want to be controlling. I don't want you to accuse me of ruining your fun. So yeah, I say it's okay. But it's not okay."

Nancy glances back and forth between Cheryl and me. She fidgets and seems to sink further into herself, like she wants to disappear. Dave continues shaking his head, the picture of put-upon. The classic nobody-understands-me posture.

"About how often do you go out, Dave?" I ask.

"I don't know. Once every couple weeks, maybe," he says.

I look at Nancy. "Does that sound right?" She is staring at Dave, eyes wide.

"You're kidding, right?" Nancy says. "Do you realize you went out three times last week alone?"

Dave is unmoved, expressionless. "I don't think so."

It's clear we're not going to get anywhere on this track. Cheryl tries a different angle.

"Nancy, when Dave tells you he's going out, how do you respond?"

"I usually don't say much. Sometimes I just say okay. Sometimes I try to be upbeat and tell him to have a good time, see you when you get home, et cetera. Once in a while I get fed up and refuse to talk to him."

"But have you ever told him honestly how it makes you feel when he goes out?" Cheryl presses.

Nancy closes her eyes for a moment and her shoulders slump. "No," she says glumly. She is all too willing to take the blame for this. And Dave is eager to let her.

"I had no idea this was bothering her so much. She never says anything." Dave's demeanor is familiar to me…his hardness, his numbness to his wife's pain. He reminds me of how Cheryl acted seventeen years ago when we were in counseling.

Cheryl and I look at each other, and we have the same thought at the same moment. Dave may be having an affair.

I decide to stop the session. I need to talk to Dave one-on-one and get to the bottom of this. He's not going to come clean with his wife in the room.

As it turns out, when I meet with Dave later and ask him if there's someone else, he admits there is. That was the first step toward healing.

Cheryl and I have seen how common it is for someone to become emotionally or physically involved with someone outside the marriage, and for their partner to be totally unaware. The spouse is in the dark, but we can see it—we almost always know when someone is having an affair.

Most of us believe that once we fall in love and marry, all is conquered. We convince ourselves that the strength of our love will override the issues that may arise. Most couples believe their marriage to be different than others, immune to failure. This is one of the most dangerous lies challenging marriages today. Cheryl and I were deceived by this thinking. We were not aware of the danger signs, so we failed to protect our own union.

Like Dave, most people are not aware of their own hardheartedness. Not at first. We have to lead them to it. They're numb to their spouses, numb to everyone else's concerns but their own. In fact, they're usually shocked when they wake up to the hardness of their own heart.

Jeff
Early 1991

We moved into the new house right after the start of the new year, five months after relocating to Dallas. One night I was upstairs reading the girls a story when the doorbell rang. I knew Cheryl was downstairs, but the doorbell kept ringing. I kept thinking, *Why isn't she answering the door?* One of the girls was asleep, but the other wasn't, so I picked her up and went downstairs to the front door.

It was the sheriff serving me with papers.

I couldn't believe it. Absolute disbelief was my first response. I didn't understand. We had just built this great house; we had these two beautiful daughters; we had an entire life together. And she was giving up that easily?

I had thought things were going better. Around the time of the move to Dallas, Cheryl had seemed in higher spirits. We hadn't talked much, but I *assumed* we were working things out. (Turned out, I frequently assumed far too many things.) I had focused on trying to be perfect for her, trying to do everything I knew to keep the family together. I wanted her to be happy, so I regularly brought her something from Nordstrom or a new piece of jewelry or a new set of golf clubs placed under the sheets on her side of the bed. I loved to see her smile. That's what the dream house was all about. Whatever it took to keep my wife happy, I'd have done it. I wanted the best for all three of my girls.

At the time I didn't realize that the best thing would have been less stuff and more of me. More of my heart, more real conversation, more serious attempts to talk to Cheryl and understand what was going on with her.

So I got those divorce papers, and after I recovered from the shock, I was angry, plain and simple. She was declaring it was over, without giving me a say in the matter. She was actually going to destroy our family.

Cheryl

I felt bad that Jeff was blindsided by the divorce papers. But I hadn't been able to get the words out. I couldn't sit with him face to face and tell him I wanted a divorce. There was a part of me that couldn't bear to hurt him that way, even though I also couldn't bear to break off my affair. Deep down, I didn't even want a divorce.

I kept going there in my mind, then I'd back off because I couldn't stand the thought of ripping apart my family. I didn't want to be with Jeff, but I didn't want to be without him either. I thought about our daughters, and I didn't want to put them through the trauma of divorce. So I was vacillating.

Todd was married too, and going through a divorce. He had no children. So he was subtly convincing me, little by little, that I needed to get out of my marriage. He'd remind me of the emptiness I felt and the relationship that he and I had built. And he'd paint a picture of a much better life, the life the girls and I could have with him. He was willing to take us on as a family. I started building a bit of resentment toward Todd because of the way he was making me feel backed into a corner. I needed to get out of my marriage, or Todd and I needed to end our relationship. Neither action seemed doable. But Todd worked to convince me there was only one real option.

I was trapped by the fact that I'd gone down this emotional road with Todd and he understandably expected me to follow through. He wanted a future with me. I had led him this far, so now I felt I owed him, in a way. It seemed unthinkable to let him down. Sadly, letting my husband down didn't seem to carry as much negative weight.

When I imagined the future, I believed that the minute I got divorced, Todd and I would be together. We would have the kind of marriage I'd dreamed of, obsessed over, for years. Our amazing connection would be played out in daily life, and I'd finally be happy. However, I couldn't grasp the logistics of how this would happen. Todd still lived in California, and we were in Texas. I was never going to take my kids away from their dad, so the only answer was for Todd to move to Dallas. We talked about it and decided to take things one step at a time. He would look into relocating and I would pursue divorce.

I pictured the fantasy of us living together in blissful romance. Sex wasn't part of the fantasy for me. It was the heart-to-heart bond. We would find a place to live in Dallas with the girls, and Jeff would somehow live down the street and be happy. What always caught me up short was whenever I thought about Jeff remarrying, I couldn't deal with it. How could I be okay with this for me, but not okay with the thought of Jeff dating someone? I couldn't imagine another woman in Jeff's life…and especially the girls' lives.

So as usual, I couldn't figure myself out. My inner dissonance was now stronger than ever. My thoughts and emotions were so contradictory that I sometimes couldn't believe they all existed within one person.

One very messed-up person.

Ironically and somewhat out of desperation, we started going to church after we settled in Dallas and while the divorce was in limbo. We attended every weekend and even joined a Sunday school class. For me, this was a new and foreign thing. I had never studied the Bible, and for some reason I was curious and interested. I had an idea, no doubt from my Catholic upbringing, that the answers to my turmoil might be found in some sort of religion or spirituality. For the first time in my life, I became consumed with curiosity about the things of God.

We were still functioning as a family, and going to church together became part of our routine. I would cry through every church service, which was strange, but I didn't have the wisdom or knowledge to understand what was happening. I just knew I was miserable, and I hoped that going to church would help me figure out what to do next.

Jeff, devastated by the course our marriage had taken, continued to beg me to work on our marriage, but to no avail. I had no interest and was still adamant about following through with the divorce, although I wasn't doing anything in particular to hurry it along. I was numb and felt emotionally and physically detached from Jeff. I was consumed by thoughts of a new life ahead of me that would be much more fulfilling.

Many times I thought about confessing the affair to Jeff. Some days I was obsessed with the idea, thinking that, if nothing else, Jeff deserved to know the truth. Other days I simply pushed it out of my mind. I was scared to death of this admission. All this turmoil was going on around me, but the worst thing I could imagine was Jeff's reaction if he found out. Fear strangled me and kept me quiet.

I began sleeping in the guest room, away from Jeff. One night after the girls were asleep and I had just gotten into bed, he came into my room and sat on the edge of my bed. His eyes were so kind and filled with tears as he looked at me. He was a heartbreaking sight...so handsome, so sad and confused.

"Cheryl, you've got to help me understand. What have I done wrong? What can I do better?"

I was so tired. I could feel his desperation, and part of me wanted to reach out to him. I wanted to give him a hug and tell him everything was going to be okay. But I was exhausted from my own emotional roller coaster, and I just couldn't deal with Jeff's questions. Maybe that was the moment I should have been confessing, but I couldn't bring myself to open my mouth.

I just looked away, shaking my head.

"Why can't we at least try?" Jeff continued. "Why do you insist on moving toward divorce? Can't you give us another chance? I haven't even had the opportunity to fix anything—you've still never told me what's wrong. Can't we work on this?"

The affair that had overtaken my heart was the elephant in the room. But he didn't see it, and I wasn't able to point it out. And without that vital piece of truth, we had nothing to talk about. The conversation couldn't go anywhere.

"Jeff," I said impatiently. "I don't want to 'work on it,' as you say. The time for work is long past. No amount of work is going to fix this."

I have to hand it to Jeff, he was incredibly persistent, blazing forward even in the face of obvious rejection.

"I'll do anything—whatever it takes to make it right," he told me.

I intentionally ignored that.

Jeff

I could not figure out what had gone so terribly wrong that Cheryl insisted on pursuing divorce. Her heart seemed to have shut down. Her mind and ears were tightly shut and locked. We continued to function day to day but didn't speak to each other about anything except the kids. The house was very large, so even when we were both home, we could easily avoid seeing each other. The extent of our relationship became the girls—we had nothing else.

Things would have made more sense if she had told me the truth. I don't know how I would have handled it. We might still have ended up divorced, because my ego was not able to handle the thought of my wife seeing someone else. But at least I would have seen things more clearly.

The way it was—with absolutely no explanation for her desperate desire to break up our family—I thought there were two possible explanations: either I was crazy, or she was. Trying to make sense out of a nonsensical situation, trying to function when the truth is kept hidden, is crazy making. At times I questioned my own perceptions, because things just didn't add up.

But I never seriously thought I was the unstable one, so the only explanation was that there was something mentally wrong with Cheryl. I'd come home from work and find her crying. Her behavior was odd, much different from our early years together. Since it never occurred to me that she would have an affair, I couldn't put it all together. I was forced to consider the possibility that Cheryl was experiencing serious psychological problems.

Worrying about Cheryl's questionable mental state made me wonder if the girls were safe with her. After our move to Dallas, Cheryl stopped working and stayed home with the twins. I was in a quandary because I didn't know if I could trust her with them. I would call during the day from work, just making sure things were okay. I started to picture Cheryl having some illness and being unable to function, and my mind was going crazy wondering, *How am I going to raise these kids by myself?* But at the same time, I was thinking, *She's always been such a good mom.* Even amid the problems we had, Cheryl had never once dropped the ball when it came to our daughters. She was devoted and conscientious. My worries about her ability to be a good mother just couldn't be right.

It got to the point where I insisted Cheryl see a psychiatrist. I needed to know, at the very least, whether our children were safe with her. She dutifully went, and nothing came of it, except that I was assured she wasn't schizophrenic or bipolar or anything like that.

But my concerns show why the truth is so important. Not knowing the truth was making me think things that weren't true. And other people agreed with me. Everyone who was counseling me at the time was telling me there was something wrong with Cheryl. But it was all because the truth wasn't revealed.

With our marriage an impending train wreck and feeling helpless to stop the raging locomotive, I needed an outlet besides my job. I dove headlong into the church. I found some degree of comfort, but mostly it was the distraction that helped me. I began reading my Bible, something I hadn't done since college. Instinctively I knew I needed something or someone beyond myself to help me get through this. Since I grew up in a Christian home, it seemed natural that when life threw me a curve ball, I turned to the faith I'd been taught. I knew there must be some kind of help in Scripture or spiritual things.

I also began working in the high school ministry, hanging out with the teenage guys, mentoring them, and leading them through Bible studies. It was a form of escape, and it helped me feel connected and needed. The detachment at home had become unbearable, and I couldn't stand the helpless feeling that defined my marriage in those days. I made friends with two married couples who also worked in the ministry, and they were the ones I could talk to about my situation. When the rest of my life was out of my control, they kept me feeling somewhat grounded.

Eighteen months after I was served with divorce papers, Cheryl walked into court and finalized it. During that entire time, I argued and begged and pleaded for her to give me another chance, but she remained obstinate. Life as I knew it was coming to an end.

SIX

Cheryl
Fall 1992

I sat on the edge of a bathtub filled with warm water and mountains of bubbles. Brittany and Lauren, four years old, splashed and played while I attempted to make sure each of them got clean.

I gazed into the soap suds and pondered our situation. I vaguely heard their belly laughs and felt the droplets flying at me like rain. My mind zipped forward to when the girls would be older. What would our divorce situation look like in the years to come? Would they get tired of being shipped from one house to another? Would resentment begin to develop even though Jeff and I got along for their sake? I wondered how the girls would understand relationships, especially when they became aware of what "really" happened in ours.

"Mommy, wash my back!" Lauren cried.

"Just a second, let me finish Brittany's hair."

"Ow! Soap in my eyes!" Brittany wailed.

"Here, let me get it." I wiped Brittany's face, washed Lauren's back, then blew soap bubbles at both of them. Giggles erupted, and soon we were in a full-scale bubble war.

"All right, girls. Time to get out. Let's rinse."

"No, Mommy, no! We wanna play!"

We played a moment longer before I helped the girls out of the tub, wrapped their warm little bodies in towels, dried their hair, and slipped them into their pajamas. We settled on the couch to cuddle and watch our favorite shows, one girl under each of my arms. This was my favorite part of the day, when the girls and I unwound together. The days felt unsettled, but in the evenings—on the nights when I had the girls—our bodies and minds seemed to relax.

This was my new life. The divorce was final, and I was finally free. Jeff and I had each bought new homes after selling the dream house. Now I was decorating bedrooms for the girls, trying to create a new feeling of home. I wanted to fashion a relaxed and homey environment for each of them in their own room. I had carefully picked out things in their favorite colors—Lauren's pink, Brittany's purple. Fluffy, cushy blankets and pillows filled these warm spaces where they could lay their heads or play house.

In some ways, I felt relieved. I still wasn't happy, but at least Jeff and I had some breathing space. I enjoyed the freedom of being in my own place, not having to pretend all the time. It was a relief to be out from under Jeff's watchful eye and be free of his never-ending pleas to save our marriage.

The girls were adjusting well to their new surroundings. They loved preschool and quickly made friends. The sad part was that so often their world would get disrupted. They would be in the middle of playing house when suddenly it would be five o'clock on a Tuesday night. Time for Jeff to pick them up and take them to his house. They could not wait to see him! But it was difficult for them to feel settled. They were always wondering where they would need to go next.

Still, laughter filled the walls of our home, and my time with the girls was the greatest blessing of my life. Most evenings after the girls were in bed or if they were at Jeff's, I'd stare unseeing at the television screen. My mind would wander. In those moments I couldn't capture the giddy feelings of freedom and relief. Tears would fill my eyes, and I'd wonder what

Jeff was doing. There was a space on the couch where he should have been.

What's wrong with me? I'd wonder. *This is what I've wanted.* Why was I still just as dissatisfied as I'd ever been?

Jeff

The day our divorce was finalized, I went to the office as usual. I had been fighting the divorce for almost two years. Cheryl was doing all the work, and I sure hadn't done anything to make it easier for her. She knew from the beginning that it wasn't what I wanted. So there was no way I was going to show up in court and give my official stamp of approval. If Cheryl was going through with it, she'd have to do it alone.

Part of me kept expecting her to come to her senses. I daydreamed that she would come up to me one day out of the blue, throw her arms around my neck, apologize, and tell me she really loved me. She'd say she had made a mistake about getting a divorce, and we would live happily ever after. Some days I fervently wished I would just wake up from this endless bad dream. I could hardly comprehend that it was my real life.

Until the last moment, when she showed up in my office with a check, I held on to the smallest hope that she'd change her mind, do an about-face, and give our marriage another chance. But instead I got "my half" of the bank account and a new identity: *Divorced man. Single dad.*

Failure.

That moment—the instant all hope was lost—changed me. I almost didn't recognize the angry, beaten guy that emerged.

The bright spot in my life was my time with Brittany and Lauren. My kids meant more to me than anything in the world, and at least Cheryl and I had been able to work out an equitable custody arrangement. The girls were with me about half the time, and I lived for those days. When they were with Cheryl and I was alone, I concentrated on my job, the youth ministry at church, and going to the gym. That was it. That was my life.

I'd never imagined I could get to a place like this. My emotions ping-ponged from seething anger at Cheryl, to hopelessness about my situation, then to dull numbness as I tried not to think about everything that had happened.

Cheryl
Late 1992–Early 1993

The first few months after the divorce went by quickly as we all tried to adjust to the unfamiliar shape of our lives. When I looked in the mirror, I thought I had lost weight (something I didn't need), and my face looked tired and drawn. I wondered why this would be. After all, I was in love!

I lived for the long-distance phone calls I could finally take without sneaking around. On average there were ten a day. The nighttime talks, after the girls were in bed or on the nights I was alone, sometimes lasted three hours or more. I don't even know what we talked about. All I know is that I got filled up emotionally. I was like a drug addict, needing my regular fix. I would get off of the phone with my emotional tank brimming over. I was satisfied and excited for the next day when it would start all over again.

Todd and I began to see each other about once a month, and sex became a natural part of the equation. In between visits, the sexual and emotional energy was intense between us on the phone.

Yet on some level I felt like I was only going through the motions. Blissful happiness was elusive. But what else could I do? This was my situation—I'd created it. There was nothing to do but keep putting one foot in front of the other and continue in the relationship with Todd. His divorce recently had been finalized. I wondered why, even though it was no longer an adulterous affair, it still didn't feel right. There was always a weird gnawing that I could not put my finger on. I was doing what I had been doing, feeding my addiction, yet my soul was distraught. Not knowing what else to do—and knowing I couldn't survive without my frequent "fixes" of ego-satisfying connection—I continued on, confident that peace and joy would eventually surface.

My dealings with Jeff were extremely strained. It was hard for Jeff to look at me or have a conversation with me. Every time we were around each other, the pain in the air could be cut with a knife. We both felt it. We were cordial because of the kids, and Jeff did a great job of acting like he was totally "over" me. I had no idea how he was feeling. He was stone faced behind his forced smile, a wall seemingly never to be penetrated. Countless times I would burst into tears after he picked up the girls or brought them home. Part of it was that I couldn't admit I missed him. But mostly, it was devastating to see Jeff—a man always so full of life and love and laughter—so quiet, numb, and expressionless. The saving grace was that he wasn't that way when he was alone with the girls. From what they told me, he was his usual happy self with them. Thank God.

"Cheryl, why don't you come to my church this Sunday? You need to get out. We can go for coffee beforehand."

My dear friend Halle had been with me through the entire divorce process. She'd been my lifeline in many ways, especially because she was so funny and lighthearted and always made me laugh. But she held my feet to the fire when necessary too. She knew about the affair, and she was trying to love me without scaring me away from Christianity. She delicately helped me see that the affair was wrong but was not sure how to convince me exactly how wrong it was. She was doing a balancing act. (I later found out Halle was furious about the affair! She regrets not having pushed me to see the devastating sin of it all. But I have to give her credit for truly showing me the love of Christ in the way she stood by me.)

"I don't know," I told her. "I don't think I'm ready for a new church." It wasn't the people I feared—I've always been social, and I love meeting new people—it was simply the idea of a new church that scared me.

"Well, you can't keep going to your old church," she reminded me. Jeff and I had started going to that church when we first moved to Dallas. For two years we'd attended, and Jeff was involved in ministry there. It had become his haven and a type of family for him as our marriage had disintegrated. The people there loved him, and when word got around that I'd left him, it became obvious that they were angry with me (understandably). It was clear that I couldn't continue going there.

I sighed. "You're right. I need to give Jeff some space. I'm not even comfortable there anymore. I feel like everyone's looking at me, like I'm wearing a huge scarlet *A* on my forehead."

"Forget about the *A*, Cheryl. But it's time to make a change. Meet me at the coffee shop at nine."

What could I say to that?

"All right, *Mom*. See you there."

I tagged along to Halle's church that Sunday, and she began introducing me to her friends. I immediately felt overwhelmed with a kindness and love I had never experienced. These strangers took me by the hand and accepted me as I was, even though my life was in shambles. Over the next few weeks as I got to know more people and shared my story, I never felt judged, only loved. Even though I was a "sinner" by the definitions of Christianity, they put their arms around me and took me in. It was almost surreal. Even the pastor and his wife were kind to me, which felt odd. Somehow I didn't expect "people like that" to accept someone like me. They were the first ones to sit with me and talk in everyday language about Jesus. I was intrigued.

I'd been raised Catholic, so I knew what sin was, but my understanding was limited. I suppose that subconsciously I thought I was a "bad" person now because of everything I had done. We'd had a good couple of years in church (the church Jeff continued to attend), but because of the extreme shunning I felt when people found out we were divorcing, my perception of myself as tainted and unforgivable was confirmed. Nobody at Jeff's church had tried to reach out to me or had asked me about my part in our story, yet the people at this new church seemed to accept me, even when they learned my situation.

I bought a Bible for the first time in my life, but didn't know what to do with it. Sure, it's a book, which means you're supposed to read it, right? I seemed to have an insatiable desire to understand it, but every time I picked it up, I felt confused. Halle helped me get involved in a Bible study, and, slowly, I began to learn to read the mysterious book I suddenly found fascinating.

I loved my new church. I sat in my same seat every week, and the name "Jesus" was spoken countless times. But one Sunday, for the very first time, I actually *heard* it. It's hard to explain, but it felt like I heard it in my heart, not just in my head. I thought I already knew who Jesus was, but I quickly realized there was more to the story. My friends told me that Jesus wanted my heart. I didn't get it but never stopped listening. What did they mean?

At the same time, my instinct was to run. I had started to adjust to my new status of being single. For the first time in many years, I was beginning to feel *satisfied* with my life. I didn't need anything (or anyone) rocking the boat. So I held back on the whole Jesus thing for a brief time. I was a little too scared to jump right in with both feet. Meanwhile, as I looked back on my failed marriage, I became curious about whether the Bible said anything about marriage, love, and relationships.

To tell the truth, I thought some of the people around me were a little kooky. They seemed to be obsessed with their religion. I'd never in my life met people like this. They were all apparently on a first-name basis with Jesus, yet they were so *normal*. They were fun people, and although they were not perfect—they still had struggles—they exuded a peace and joy I could not fathom. A peace and joy I realized I'd never had.

It slowly dawned on me that this Jesus everyone was talking about could be what I'd been missing. I learned he could be my Savior and that *Savior* wasn't just some fancy religious word; it meant he could literally save my life. What? Where had I been? Why had this been so foreign to me? Gradually I began to grasp that I had a choice to make, a decision that would change my life forever.

I sat in my comfy living-room recliner, as I'd grown accustomed to doing early in the morning when I read the Bible. I took a deep breath.

"Okay." I spoke aloud. I knew Jesus heard me. I was giving my life to him, even though I still wasn't quite sure what that meant. I felt like a little child when I went on, "Jesus, forgive me of my sins and be the Lord of my life."

The best way I can describe what happened at that moment was that it felt like a boulder had been lifted off me.

I felt my body relax, and I seemed to be able to breathe easier (although I'm sure I did not breathe any differently than I had before). For months I had existed in a near-constant state of anxiety. But over the next few days, my body seemed to be moving in slow motion. At the same time, I felt invigorated and had more energy. Even my voice was calmer.

Emotionally I moved to a more even keel. I stopped crying so much. I felt like I had someone to lean on (Jesus!). I felt as though I had somewhere to turn with my emotions (prayer!)...someone to cry out to in the pain. In the midst of all the turmoil, I felt peace and joy in a way I'd never experienced in my life. I realized then that I had never lived with a sense of peace.

It was all new, and in some ways I felt like a silly stereotype. How could this really be happening?

It seemed there was a deeper purpose to life, and I wanted to find out what it was. My mind was clearer and more focused. The hole in my life was being filled for the first time. It felt like freedom. I did not understand the path I was about to take, but was willing to do my best to walk down it.

As it happened, another friend of mine, Marci, told me about a local Monday night Bible study. The average attendance normally hit a thousand people, but the first night I attended, three thousand showed up. The speaker was Tommy Nelson, senior pastor of Denton Bible Church, and as I began to listen, my mouth dropped open. He was teaching a series on the Song of Solomon from the Old Testament. I had only just heard of this book the week before, when someone told me it was about God's plan for a man-woman relationship and marriage.

For six weeks I sat nearly disbelieving as I listened to Tommy Nelson. He was teaching that God intended us to experience deep emotional, sexual, and spiritual satisfaction in marriage. He spoke about keeping romance alive, about growing closer together while resolving conflicts, about treating each other with respect. He explained how a marriage with God at the center looked completely different from a "worldly" or godless relationship. He was talking about a marriage filled with greater love, joy, and commitment than I'd ever known. I felt numb as it dawned on me that Jeff and I had lived our marriage very far from God's plan. I had not even known God had a specific plan for marriage. This was all new to me. Relationships, God-style.

God had a style? Who knew! I dove into the study alone, reading the book between the weekly sessions. Ironically, I was busting at the seams to tell Jeff. But I never said a word to him because I knew he didn't want to hear anything from me, especially about *us*. He was moving on with his life. He had worn himself out fighting for our marriage and had lost. The last thing he wanted to hear was what "God was doing in my life" and what I thought God was telling me.

One evening as I studied deeper in the Song of Solomon, I felt a funny sort of resentment creep its way inside my soul. I had been raised Catholic and attended Mass nearly every Sunday of my childhood. In the first two years we lived in Dallas, I'd been to church countless times. Why had I never heard this stuff? Why had the pulpit been devoid of this incredible news? Thirty-three years of my life had slipped by without me knowing that God had a design for marriage. I felt like I was just beginning to see the mess my life had been.

I sank down in my chair, put down my Bible, and covered my face with my hands. *Why, God?* my heart cried out. *Why have I wasted so much of my life?* There was no answer. I sat there—I don't know how long—too sad even for tears.

The evenings took on a new rhythm. If I didn't have the girls, I spent most of the time praying and studying the Bible. If the girls were with me, I'd settle into my chair after they went to bed. One night as I continued to try to understand the beautiful poetry of the Song of Solomon, the strangest feeling came over me—a foreign sensation that I was *not alone*. I stood and stared at myself in the mirror. My body trembled as a sense of awe overtook me.

There are no accidents. The realization filled me. *I didn't end up at the Bible study by coincidence.* Could it be that God had placed me there on purpose? That he'd sent Marci specifically to invite me, because he had things to show me? I never thought God worked that way. But this was unmistakable, a deep knowing.

Suddenly it seemed there was this whole other side of life I had no idea about—and that God actually had it all spelled out. How could this be true? I can't even see God! I was coming to grips with the fact that God is so huge and does such incomprehensible things. I was starting to think I could believe he did have a plan, if I would just open my heart to it. The awe was in realizing that I did not have to spend the rest of my life trying to do it on my own like I had my first thirty-three years.

Somehow I was sure that Someone was trying to tell me something. And I thought he was trying to tell me that I'd done everything all wrong. That I never should have divorced Jeff. That our marriage could have been so different—so much better—than it was.

I tried to shake off the feeling. That was all well and good, but Jeff and I were already divorced. I had moved forward with my life—and Todd was still in the picture. In fact, we were seeing each other more than ever. Whatever God was trying to tell me about my marriage to Jeff, it was too late. There was nothing I could do.

Somewhere in the middle of the Tommy Nelson study, my confusion led me to seek out a Christian counselor. I was a little scared, remembering my previous unsuccessful counseling experiences. But I was determined to be honest this time. Maybe if I did, Ryan could help me. I sat fidgeting on one end of the sofa in his office.

"That's quite a story," Ryan admitted after I'd explained everything the best I could. I just nodded as I felt my cheeks flush.

"I have to be honest with you," he continued. "If you want healing in your life, it's going to take a lot of work."

I nodded again.

"You'll need to spend a great deal of time journaling and getting face to face with yourself. We need to meet at least once a week, probably for several months. Do you think you're up for it?"

"I do." My voice was firm, although my shaking hands may have betrayed my lack of confidence. I liked how Ryan seemed ready and willing to go through this with me. His strength began to rub off on me, and I told him, "I can't keep living with this feeling of failure and not knowing what to do next. I've got to get my life on track."

He considered me with his head tilted, seeming to gauge whether I was capable of this commitment.

"You can always change your mind. Just because you're here doesn't mean you have to move forward right now. You might want to wait until you're feeling stronger."

"No." I shook my head. "No, now's the time. Let's get started."

It seemed God was working overtime sending people to help me. I figured the least I could do was go along for the ride.

So week after week, I listened to sermons, learned more about the Bible, listened to Tommy Nelson speak, and went to counseling. Whenever my daughters were at school or with Jeff, I was deep into this journey that was more spiritual and more personal than I'd ever thought possible. I was seeing the truth about myself for the first time, and more importantly, I was getting to know the ways of God.

~

This is where I'm supposed to live happily ever after, right? Well, I was human (still am) and a long way from any semblance of spiritual maturity. So even after this new revelation and change of direction in my life, I continued the long-distance relationship with Todd. There was no lightning bolt from the sky that struck me and said I should stop, and emotionally I was incredibly dependent on him. A void was being filled by this man, and I was still a long way from knowing how to seek God to satisfy my empty places.

Something in me whispered that this relationship that had begun in adultery was not right for me. That God had a better plan. That I needed to break up with Todd so that my healing could continue.

Of course, it wasn't just a still, small voice within—Ryan, my counselor, said it to me out loud plenty of times. Marci suggested it. Halle brought it up. For whatever reason, everyone seemed convinced that my road to recovery did not include Todd. I would wake up each day committed to following Jesus and doing the right thing and determined to end the relationship. Then the phone would ring, I'd hear his voice, and I'd be sunk.

Why the obsession? What was the draw? After all this time, Todd was still the only one who made me feel like a princess and the most beautiful woman in the world. He *understood* me, and what I was about. I didn't want to give this up and fought with all I had to preserve it.

God was transforming me one minute at a time. I could not get enough of the Bible. It was consuming me. Every free moment I had, I was reading and absorbing Scripture. I was journaling all the time and facing my sin. Yet I was also coming up against the brick wall of my own stubbornness. I still wanted things *my way.* I did not want to give up my soul mate. Everything in me told me my affair with Todd was right, but it seemed God was telling me it was wrong.

I began to pray for God to take away my feelings for Todd. I asked God to bring me to a place of peace and confidence where I could live without Todd. My heart was torn, but God was winning out. I knew I had to walk away from this man, but I had no idea how I was going to do it. The pull was greater than any I had ever experienced in my life.

And out of nowhere came the thought: *What if I'm supposed to go back to Jeff?*

Ryan looked at me with something resembling disbelief.

"Are you thinking of trying to reconcile with your husband?"

I nodded.

"Maybe we need to slow down here. You're just starting to get some perspective on your situation. Let's not jump ahead." Ryan's cautiousness surprised me.

"But I'm taking responsibility here. I'm admitting it was my fault. This was all wrong—every bit of it. I shouldn't have had the affair. I shouldn't have insisted on divorce. I was selfish and…and…*wrong.*"

"You're right, Cheryl, but that's just the beginning. You're not ready for this. Have you spent much time thinking about how Jeff might feel about this?"

"Of course. But once he sees how I've changed, things will be different. Look at me. I'm a whole new person."

Ryan was quiet for a couple of moments, just looking at me. I started to squirm. His silence was never a good thing.

What was I missing?

Scenes flashed in my mind. Jeff pleading with me to give the marriage a chance. Me sneaking off to talk to Todd. The girls being shuttled back and forth between two homes. Jeff's face when I handed him the check after the divorce was final. A family ripped apart, a beautiful life ruined.

The devastation I'd left in my wake. *Oh, God. God help me. What have I done?*

"I'm still being selfish." It was a statement, not a question, said with my eyes on the floor.

"Are you?" Ryan's voice was kind.

"I need to apologize." I looked up. "To Jeff."

My heart was heavy when I thought of how hard this would be. I spent the next two months figuring out what words could possibly express my sorrow for the pain I'd caused my family.

SEVEN

Jeff
1993

The first few months after the divorce were brutal. I couldn't get used to being alone. All I'd ever wanted was to be a great husband, a great dad, the true family guy. I suddenly found myself paying child support and dealing with a visitation schedule. I couldn't adjust to the fact that half the time my kids were somewhere else. The pain in my gut just never went away. It was almost physical much of the time, a twisting, aching sensation somewhere beneath my ribs.

My life was filled with peaks and valleys—highs when I had the girls and lows when I did not have them. Brittany and Lauren were with me the first, third, and fifth weekends of the month and two consecutive nights during the week. It varied every other week—when I had them on the weekend, I had them Wednesday and Thursday nights. When Cheryl had them on weekends, I had them Monday and Tuesday nights.

When they stayed with me, I took them to school. On a typical day with the girls, I would get them up, make them breakfast, help them get dressed, pack their lunches, get them to school (which was near Cheryl's house) and then head to work. If it was my night for them, I would either go back over to Cheryl's house and pick them up, or if they had an activity (T-ball, art, piano, gymnastics, dance), pick them up from there, make them dinner, play with them, help them with their homework, and get them to bed to be ready for the next day at school. When I didn't have the girls for the night, I would usually work out, come home, eat, go to a friend's house or a youth function, come home and watch TV, then go to bed.

The weekends without the girls were the worst part for me. I had bought a lake house, so if it was summer, I would often go to the lake, hang out with friends, or do things with the youth group.

Seeing Cheryl when we exchanged the kids was the worst. I carried my anger like a trophy, right out in front. It defined me. Most of the time I actually felt like I hated her. I was careful never to say a single negative thing about Cheryl to the kids, and I was always as polite as I could be. But I never looked directly at her, and we never spoke about anything except the girls.

"Brittany's got a dentist appointment."

"Did you sign those school papers?"

"Lauren's game starts at six."

"Parent-teacher conferences are next week."

"Their new swimsuits are in their backpacks."

So when Cheryl called and asked if she could come over to talk to me, I wasn't having any of it.

"Why can't you just tell me over the phone? Is it about the girls?"

"No," Cheryl said. "It's…something else."

"Then, no. I don't want to talk." I wanted to add, *We had years to talk, and you never wanted to*. But I didn't.

"Jeff, please. It will only take twenty minutes, I promise."

Once again Cheryl was stubbornly getting her way with me. I sighed, not having the energy to argue with her.

"Fine. Twenty minutes."

When she arrived, she could barely look me in the face and her eyes filled with tears. She went immediately to the bathroom, then came out, her face a bit puffy. I'd seen it all before and felt nothing.

"Is it okay if I sit beside you?" she asked. What nerve.

"No, Cheryl. I'm sitting here. You sit there." I pointed to the chair across the room. I didn't want to be so callous, but I was completely uncomfortable with this whole thing. She sat and pulled some papers out of her bag—quite a few pages, it seemed.

"I wrote you a letter," she said haltingly. "And I wanted to read it to you." Inwardly I groaned. I guessed she was going to apologize. *About time*, I thought, but I didn't want to hear it. I was not going to get emotional about anything. But I felt as though I had to listen, almost out of guilt. After all, she'd taken the time to write this thing. I wasn't interested in anything she had to say, but I listened out of a sense of obligation or duty.

Cheryl began reading the letter to me. It was extremely long, but I was blocked with resentment and irritation and I only comprehended snippets.

"Dear Jeff,

"I want you to know that this is taking a lot for me to sit here and pour my heart out to you. I have wanted to do this for a long time but never seemed to find the courage to do so…"

I leaned back in my chair and crossed my arms. This might be worse than I thought.

"Jeff, first I want to start out with apologies. Some of these things burden me every day, and I need to tell you how truly sorry I am. I am so sorry for the deep hurt I have caused you. I never intentionally meant to hurt you…

"I am very sorry I never opened up to you during our marriage. I was scared and felt insecure about some of my thoughts and especially some of my feelings. I wish I had reached out more to you and given you a chance to listen. I am sorry for not letting you know my true feelings and what I was thinking. It was not fair to you. I wanted more than anything to open up; I just did not know how…

"I truly regret and apologize for giving up… I'm sorry for not enduring and working through hard times. I'm sorry for not treating you with respect, and I'm sorry for not listening when you were trying to get through to me. I'm sorry for shutting you out, and I'm sorry for being selfish."

I closed my eyes and clamped down my teeth. I had plenty of good comebacks, but now was not the time to interrupt. She was on a roll.

"You know, Jeff, I have so many unanswered questions in my mind that play over and over again. I hope that one day you could give me the answers. I know this sounds like a weird question, but did you truly love me? The reason I ask this is because although you told me so often that you loved me, I did not feel you liked me very well. You were so critical, judgmental, and distant. What did you love about me? I honestly do not even know…

"I had never thought divorce would be an option in my life. But I was so emotionally and physically starved for you… You have no idea how much. Divorce seemed the only answer. I felt I was constantly failing you. I did not feel understood and walked around with knots in my stomach from needing your attention and love…"

I looked at the ceiling, then at the floor. Anywhere but at Cheryl.

"I know you did not expect it, but I wanted to be the perfect wife for you. I felt as though I was a good wife and thought I was doing all the right things, but I did not feel you thought that. I wanted your approval, respect, admiration, affection, and love.

"I want forgiveness from you. I have forgiven you for the hurts you caused me. I want to heal… I especially want you to heal and be free from all the wounds on your heart. I feel we both had so much hurt that we were unable to reach out to each other. I feel so sad, because what a waste it is…

"There are so many times I miss our family being together. I think about you a lot and miss you… However, I do not miss our past relationship. It was damaging for both of us.

"I had and sometimes still do have dreams regarding us as a couple…
I wanted so much for us. I wanted you to be my best friend, yet I did not
feel close to you. It was very frustrating to me. I did not know how to get
close to you or talk to you. I thought I did, but what I tried did not seem
to be effective. So I basically tried to ignore the situation and be a good
wife. Believe me, Jeff, I'm not saying this was the right way, it was just the
only way I knew…"

My foot started tapping, and I forced it to stop. I stifled a yawn. Was
she almost finished?

"Sometimes I feel like I did not give our relationship enough time…

"Sometimes I wish I had another chance, but I'm so afraid it would be
like it was.

"You know, Jeff, believe it or not, I pray for us every day. I pray for our
situation and ask God to show me what he wants for my life. I do not have
peace with what has happened to us. It just isn't settled in my heart and mind.
My heart is still so much with you. I know you may not want to hear this,
as you appear to have gotten on with your life and appear to be happy…

"There are times when I really miss you…

"I am sorry for being selfish with you and trying to solve everything on
my own.

"Jeff, I always loved you and probably always will.

"Jeff, you may think differently, but I always loved you."

It was over. *Phew.*

As she came to the end of the letter, she paused and took a deep breath.
She explained that she had been going to church, reading the Bible, and
had become a Christian.

What's that saying? How *convenient*.

Then she asked if I would ever consider giving us another chance. I squinted at her as if she had suddenly become an alien. Was she for real? She seemed so hopeful and confident that it almost broke my heart again.

Almost.

I'll admit I did get slightly tearful. It was all just too much. Or maybe too little, too late. I cleared my throat.

"Cheryl," I began, in the kindest tone I could muster. "I appreciate your coming over. But I'm never going to be open to the idea. I wasn't the one who destroyed our marriage, and I gave you plenty of chances to come around while we were still married. Please don't ever—*ever*—bring this up again." I stood up.

She looked stunned. Her eyes filled again, while I simply stood there looking at her. Finally she rose, and I herded her toward the door.

"Cheryl, I appreciate your repentance. I forgive you. Let's not talk about this ever again. We need to be civil to one another for the girls—but that's it. No more."

I held the door for her, and she scooted out. *Don't let the door hit you...*

I stood in my living room for I don't know how long. How dare she? How dare she? Haven't I been through enough already? Does she think she can keep whipping me around like this?

And becoming a Christian. Yeah, right. How very nice for her. I didn't believe it for a second. Cheryl needed absolution. But I wasn't the one to give it to her.

Cheryl

Being booted out the door was not part of the plan.

My ears buzzed and my head spun. What had just happened? I was barely aware of leaving the porch of Jeff's new house and walking to my car. It was one of those drives home where I looked up and suddenly I was in my own driveway and couldn't remember how I'd gotten there.

Two hours later, I lay in bed wide awake, struggling with having to forever live with the consequences of my decision to rip my family apart. I was so frustrated with myself, and with God, that I just wanted to kick something! Why did he wait so long to get my attention? This whole mess could have been avoided.

During the couple of months I was preparing the letter for Jeff, my emotions vacillated wildly. I knew I needed to apologize, but I kept thinking God was telling me more. I kept having a vision of our marriage restored. It was impossible to wrap my mind around it. To be honest, when I thought about the energy, work, determination, and time it might take to carry this out, I quickly backed away. I still kept hearing it, or feeling it, or whatever it was—the nudge toward reconciliation. Was this just my guilt talking?

Frankly, I had no desire to pursue the mission God was birthing. It seemed impossible, impractical, and unachievable. Going backward didn't jive with the new life I was striving for. Several times, I made up my mind to ignore God.

But God wasn't ignoring me! So I kept on doggedly drafting that letter to Jeff, not sure it would ever see the light of day, but feeling better for putting my feelings on paper anyway. I wrestled day after day with this, wondering why I was going to so much trouble, until God slapped me in the face with a whole new thought: this was not about me, it was about God and his desires for my life and my family's life.

Huh. I'd never thought of it that way. Did God have a particular plan for me? I didn't know whether to believe it, but I'd already committed my life to him, so I needed to consider it. After more wrestling with my fear and pride, I made a pledge to God that I would try to understand what he wanted me to do and try to follow.

So the day I read the letter to Jeff in his living room, I "just knew" he'd be on the same page as me. I knew I was following God's plan and Jeff's heart would be touched. I was nervous reading the letter aloud but excited too. When I finally finished, I looked up and the tears in Jeff's eyes confirmed my expectations.

But as soon as Jeff spoke, everything changed. I'd never heard him so polite or so firm. "Here's the door. Leave," was how it sounded to me.

So maybe I'd misunderstood what God was trying to tell me those past few months. Maybe I'd gotten it all wrong. Clearly, reconciliation was not the answer. Did this mean I was supposed to continue in my *other* relationship? I hadn't broken it off yet; I was still hedging my bets, not knowing how Jeff would respond to my letter.

I agonized back and forth. What to do? Where to go from here? I heard that now-familiar voice again.

I am in control, Cheryl.

I desperately wanted to believe God was in control but lacked the faith. I remembered my mom telling me, "You kids. You never want to work hard at things." And suddenly I realized she was right. Following God in this—pursuing restoration of my marriage—would be really hard. And I didn't think I was up for it.

In many ways, I kept trying to control things myself. Since Jeff was not an option, I kept talking to Todd and seeing him occasionally. It was a couple of weeks later, I was talking to Todd on the phone, and he noticed I was distracted.

"Cheryl, are you there?"

"Sure, sure. What were you saying?"

"I asked if a week from Saturday would be okay for my next trip to Dallas."

I glanced at the calendar that held the details of the girls' schedule. It jarred me to think of my daughters and Todd at the same time. I didn't like the combination.

"That weekend looks fine. What do you want to do?"

"How about we look at houses? It might not be too long until I can transfer."

Houses. I thought of the dream house Jeff and I had shared with the girls. For a moment the memory melded with something that seemed like a vision of the future...I saw Jeff and me together in the house, with the girls a little older...

"Cheryl?"

What was I doing? Making plans with Todd, dreaming of Jeff... I shook it off.

"Todd, I need to go."

"What... Why?"

"It's okay, everything's fine, I just need to go. Talk to you tomorrow?"

I hung up the phone, and I sat there trying to understand my own head and heart.

I began to comprehend that maybe this relationship was filling me up in some kind of counterfeit way, that it was not the real thing. But I couldn't pull back. Todd and I had talked about marriage, and I had begun to convince myself that this could be God's plan.

The truth is, I was trying hard to believe that Todd was the right direction when my heart was telling me otherwise. Peace filled me when I thought of Jeff. Turmoil clouded my mind when I thought of a future with Todd. But I kept trying to talk myself into making Todd the right choice.

So the pursuit of restoring my marriage took the back burner, along with the deepest truth of my heart.

⁓

Despite my obvious turmoil and my persistent inability to make the right choice, my friends were fantastic. The days when I didn't have the girls were difficult, but my girlfriends were always there for me. We'd frequently hang out at each other's homes or go out to dinner together. The conversations and support kept me sane.

One night Marci and I made dinner in her kitchen. I fumbled for words, trying to explain my crazy and constant emotional flip-flops.

"The problem is, even though Jeff slammed the door in my face, I keep thinking God is still telling me that we're going to reconcile. Then I face the facts, realize it's not going to happen, and I'm back to thinking I'm going to marry Todd. But every time I talk to Todd these days, I think of Jeff."

Marci thought for a moment. "Do you feel peace when you're talking to Todd?"

"Yes….no….um." Which was it? "No, I don't. I feel emotionally soothed. Like for the moment, everything is okay. But the minute I hang up the phone, it disappears, and I can't wait until the next time we talk."

"And what about when you're thinking about Jeff? Imagining getting your marriage back?"

I remembered the day Jeff sat on my bed, pleading with me to talk to him. He was so sweet and caring, and even though I rudely rebuffed him, I felt he would have done anything in his power for me right then. Could getting my marriage back be a real possibility?

But then I flashed on Jeff's face after I'd read him the letter—the coldness, the way he seemed utterly devoid of feeling for me. No, he'd never forgive me. I'd never forgive myself, actually. Yet the truth was there.

"When I think about Jeff, it's the only time I feel absolutely peaceful. I don't know why, since he isn't going to come around. It doesn't make sense."

"Okay," Marci said. "So you don't feel peaceful with Todd, but you're thinking about marrying him."

"I know; it's crazy!" I confessed. "Maybe it's because I just don't know how to stop the train. I don't know how to get off."

"I wonder." Marci paused for a minute. "I wonder if your kids are the key."

"What do you mean?" I asked.

"Can you imagine Todd being in the house with them…being the one to raise them with you?"

My stomach dropped as though I were on a roller coaster. I thought of Todd's last visit, when he'd come to the house to see me and the girls. He had invaded Jeff's territory, and it didn't work. I didn't want him around my girls—it was so unnatural. No one could take Jeff's place.

God help me. "You're right. I don't know if I can do this."

While I was distraught over the whole situation with Jeff and Todd, the one thing that seemed to bring consistent peace was the time I spent trying to know and understand God. I rose every morning at five. I'd brew the coffee and savor the scent permeating the room. The silence and darkness brought a peaceful anticipation. I'd grab my cup, pour the coffee, then retreat to my favorite cozy chair that had become a refuge of sorts over the last few months. This was the time for me to read the Bible, and this was where I learned to pray.

For the first time in my life I was learning to listen to my heart and understand myself. I was getting comfortable in my own skin and having confidence in God. This is where I began to truly understand a relationship with Jesus—that it was him speaking into my life. I was never sure why I decided to listen. Does anyone understand why they succumbed to the voice of God? I was *contemplating* life for the first time, instead of just *doing* life.

I'd sit for a few minutes and quiet my mind and heart. I wrote whatever came to my mind—my thoughts, feelings, frustrations, and needs. Then I waited. When I sensed God trying to tell me something, I wrote it down. After a few weeks of this, it dawned on me that this is a conversation with God! So much of what I was hearing was his voice leading and directing me.

At first, I did not understand "time alone with God" or spending hours in prayer by myself. Up to this point, my knowledge of prayer was the rosary—Our Fathers and Hail Marys said over and over again. It was a novelty to think I could talk directly to God as if he were a friend. I couldn't fathom God having a personal interest in me, my life, my struggles. My first real experience with this kind of prayer was in the small groups and Bible studies I was attending. But as I spent more and more time in my chair, I came to crave time alone with God. Sometimes hours would go by as I wrestled with the Lord, and I would not even realize it. Sometimes I would look back over the tussling, and I'd find I'd written twenty pages in my journal.

It was like an out-of-body experience. I was sure God was sitting with me—he was in the room for sure—sometimes sitting in my chair with me.

He challenged me with statements and questions. I wrote them down and dialogued back and forth with him on my paper. I was oblivious to my surroundings. It was like all that existed was me, my chair, my coffee cup, and God. Then I would "wake up" and think, *Oh gosh, I need to get started with my day.* I truly went to a different place during these times.

One morning, a few weeks after Jeff had refused my suggestion of reconciliation, I spent a particularly chaotic wrestling session in my chair. I'd been writing frantically in my journal. I read back over what I had just written and sat stunned. I could barely breathe.

"Pursue putting your marriage back together, Cheryl."

What? I reread it several times. Had I really written that?

I could hear the words reverberating in my head as if they'd been spoken. I opened and shut my eyes quickly, trying to focus on the page. It was surreal. I knew the words were not my own because I was far from believing in the idea of putting the marriage back together.

I threw the journal on the floor.

I wasn't sure I liked this God stuff, this pursuit of Jesus. *Difficult* is an understatement. It made me crazy. None of it made sense. I was challenged beyond my capability.

It made me want to go back to controlling things myself. I was constantly flipping back and forth. I don't know how God was so patient with me. If I were God, I would have walked away from me! He would be quiet for a time, then bombard me again, reminding me to pray for the reconciliation of my marriage. Occasionally a shimmer of hope shone through; Jeff calling me or randomly asking if we could all ride to a T-ball game together. But emotionally we were on different planes: I was inching toward considering a relationship with him, while he was closed off, only dealing with me for the sake of the girls. For the most part, we repelled each other like water and oil.

Jeff

During the weeks and months following Cheryl's reading of the letter, things settled into a new kind of normal. I remained distant from her and mostly I just felt numb. Maybe I was working hard to avoid feeling anything. I used all my energy trying to manage my new life, take care of the girls, work at my job, and spend time with the youth group. I wasn't interested in dating yet, and I was celibate, which wasn't any fun since I'd been used to regular intimacy in marriage. But while it may have been difficult, it didn't matter much to me. The most important thing in my life was my daughters.

Our custody arrangements were working out fine, and Cheryl and I never had any problems with them. We seemed to easily cooperate when it came to taking care of the girls. Their schedule was sometimes hectic, with sports and other activities, and occasionally I needed to travel for business. But whatever happened, we always worked it out. As a result, Cheryl and I talked at least a couple of times a day, and we saw each other several times a week, if not more.

Brittany and Lauren were well loved and well cared for, and they felt it. But sometimes bedtime was very hard. When the girls were at my house, they missed Cheryl. And when they were with Cheryl, they missed me. Occasionally one of them (or both) would cry inconsolably. On a number of occasions, I went over to Cheryl's at bedtime to tuck the girls in and stay until they fell asleep. And sometimes she came over to my place to do the same. It didn't change things between us. But at least the kids knew they could count on us.

Then one day I walked up to Cheryl's house to pick up the girls. She never had anyone over when I was there, but this day she did. I recognized him as Todd, a guy I'd met years before and seen at several of Cheryl's work-related functions when we lived in California. I quickly gathered Brittany and Lauren, and we were out of there before Todd even had a chance to say hello.

But instantly, everything clicked into place.

Later I asked the girls if they knew Todd. They didn't have much to say, except that he was Mommy's friend and they'd seen him a few times. Unbelievable. This was the guy. This was the reason we'd gone through all this. *How long has it been going on?* I wondered. How could I have been so stupid?

I already carried around anger at Cheryl, so I don't think that got any worse. I wasn't even jealous, except for the fact that I didn't want anyone else raising my kids. Ironically, the thing I remember feeling is relief. It was a huge "aha" moment, when everything started to make sense. I felt vindicated. I hadn't been crazy after all—I'd known there was more to Cheryl's story than she was telling me.

But after the relief subsided, the sense of betrayal took on huge new proportions. How could she have been so disloyal? So utterly dismissive of me? So entirely disrespectful of who I was as a man, as her husband, as the father of her children?

The magnitude of Cheryl's dishonesty was nearly incomprehensible. At least I was convinced beyond a doubt of one thing: besides our kids, she and I had nothing to talk about ever again.

Cheryl
Spring 1994

As I continued studying the Bible, praying, and journaling, gradually I started feeling an insatiable desire to be around Jeff as much as possible. I started missing him when several days had gone by and I had not seen him.

My heart was stirring with emotions I barely recognized. An inkling of my love for Jeff that had died many years before was resurfacing. Nearly two years had passed since I'd first started journaling with God, and now I found myself praying for Jeff every day and praying for the reconciliation of our marriage.

It didn't really make sense to me, but I was starting to realize it was a spiritual thing. It was a God movement. He was pouring into me, teaching me, and changing my heart. He was giving me a love for Jeff again. I fought it because I still didn't really *want* to love him again. But I was beginning to get pictures in my mind of what it could be like with Jeff (a healthy, fulfilling, flourishing relationship) and with an intact family. For a long time I did not desire him sexually, but that began to bud as well. I was longing to be married to him again. I didn't know yet if I truly "loved" him, but I knew God was moving my heart toward Jeff.

It took effort not to call him all the time or find ways to be around him. I even made up random questions to ask him about the girls. I knew it was the only reason he would talk to me. Eye contact became a regular happening between us. The girls, now six years old, finagled ways for us to be in the same place at the same time. If Jeff and I were standing talking to each other at the exchange of the kids, they would jump between us and pull our hands closer to try to get us to hold hands; if they were riding to an event with one of us, they would ask if the other parent could ride in the same car. They would run off if we were all together so that it would be just the two of us standing or sitting together. It was classic *Parent Trap*, and we both found it amusing, but I always wondered if Jeff found it really annoying.

It took me awhile longer to disengage completely from the other relationship. It's hard to explain the addiction aspect, but like someone hooked on heroin or crack, I kept going back, no matter how much the relationship contradicted what I wanted in my life. I finally recognized the need to pray for myself. I petitioned God to eliminate the desirability, fascination, and attraction this other man held for me. But it didn't go away immediately.

Since Jeff was still as cold as ever to me, I kept losing hope we would ever be together again. That would push me right back to Todd. When Todd and I talked about our future, I felt incapable of setting him straight. Just as I had never been able to speak the truth to Jeff, now I wasn't able to speak the truth to Todd either. He finally sold his house and moved to Dallas.

My soul wrestled day in and day out. One day I felt God grabbing my attention like never before. My journal entry for that day went something like this:

> *Dear Jesus, here I am again today. Why do you keep badgering me with the idea of reconciliation? I just want to get on with my life. I'm tired and worn out.*
>
> *Cheryl, I'm sorry, but there's something you need to know. A short time ago you said you genuinely desired to surrender to me and follow my commands for your life. You did say that, right?*
>
> *Yep.*
>
> *Then you must understand this is not going to be easy. Did I ever promise you it would be easy?*
>
> *No.*
>
> *But, Cheryl, I do promise you great blessing if you hang in there. I hate to be so blunt, but you must comprehend this is not about you but about my desires for your life and your family's life. This is about my glory, not yours. Do you hear me? Are you in or not?*

I put down my pen. Tears filled my eyes. How could I be so rude to God? How could I be so selfish to think this was all about me?

I really did feel as though God was speaking through my pen. I had the sense it wasn't me doing the writing, and I truly believe this is what kept me in the game when I did not think I could continue the pursuit. It was my chair, my pen, my journal, me, and my God. At times, I felt like this was all I had. On this particular day, what he said truly pierced my heart.

After months of trying to fight my own battle by myself, I got down on my knees and cried out to the Lord.

"You got me, God. I'm done; I'm helpless. I can't do it anymore." It was no longer about what I wanted; it was about what God wanted. "I'm going to do whatever needs to be done. Whatever you tell me." I begged God to show me his way, his path, and asked him to take away any feelings I had for this other man. I promised him I was committed to surrender.

Several days later, I woke up and felt like my heart and emotions were free from the relationship with Todd. I didn't trust it at first, mainly because I didn't trust myself, but as time passed, I knew I was healed. I told Todd it wasn't going to work. I told him I was done and that I didn't love him, that the relationship was over. He was devastated. Just six months before we had been looking at engagement rings and houses. He'd been living in Dallas for only two weeks, but he packed up and went home. I knew that was the end of it.

All I could think about was Jeff. The man who could still barely stand the sight of me.

Umm...God? What next?

EIGHT

Cheryl
2007

It's a beautiful spring day, and Jeff and I are visiting friends in Colorado. We sit outside a coffee shop with Laura, talking about these events of more than a decade ago. It brings back the long years when Jeff and I were divorced and didn't know what the future held. Sometimes I feel light-years beyond those times—like they were another lifetime or another person lived it. But every once in a while, they feel fresh again, and I experience the heartbreak and confusion as if it were yesterday. That's what happens today as I listen to the pain in Laura's voice.

She has gone through the same things I experienced all those years ago. She perceived her marriage as sad, lonely, and unfulfilling. She was vulnerable and succumbed to temptation with an affair. She didn't get divorced—thank God, she pursued reconciliation before it went that far. Her marriage is a few years into restoration, and it seems to be going well—miraculously well, she admits. She is blessed with a husband who was willing to forgive, to take her back, and to seriously commit to creating a better marriage in which they can both be happy.

"The thing is, Cheryl, every time I think things are going great between John and me, something happens that makes me wonder if we'll ever be over it. Like, I'll tell him I need to go on a business trip, and he gets worried, doesn't want me to go. He's afraid it will happen again. And it's hard for me to explain to him how far beyond that I am!"

Jeff leans forward. "I know how he feels though. I was so angry at Cheryl for going that far without ever putting any effort into us. I couldn't believe she'd taken such a drastic step—looking for someone else, doing things in secret, being disloyal. It hurt so much because she did it all behind my back. For a long time I couldn't look her in the eye because of it."

"I know I wounded him deeply," Laura says sadly. "I pray every day for his heart to heal. Sometimes it seems so…hopeless. Are we going to live this way forever?"

"But Laura," I tell her. "You're just a couple of years into your restoration process. You're together and working on the marriage—but that doesn't mean things are always going to be perfect. It takes time for people to heal. For Jeff and me it was seven years."

Laura's eyes widen. "Seven years…that's *it*," she says. "Wow—I wasn't thinking of it that way. It seems like we've been back together a long time and things should be much better by now. But it hasn't been that long. I still need to be patient. I haven't given it enough time."

Jeff and I nod, and I tell her, "You may not have to wait as long as we did. Or, sorry to say, it could take longer. But if you're faithfully following God the best you know how, I think you'll see the blessing. I believe John will be healed, and your marriage will be better than ever."

"As long as I'm obedient to God."

"Yep," I tell her. "That's the key. But you're already doing that." Laura nods as I continue.

"You've been learning about God's plan for marriage, you've committed to your husband, and you've decided there's no escape clause in your marriage. Even though it's hard, and sometimes you wonder if you can do it, you keep going because you believe it's what God wants. I think with that kind of obedience, you'll be blessed."

Laura has tears in her eyes.

"You guys…your story really helps. If you could wait so many years for reconciliation, I guess I can keep being patient. For as long as it takes. At least I'm still married—I have to believe John's heart will be healed. And trust he won't always be so worried."

"And he's going to get there by watching *you*," Jeff chimes in. "The more he's able to see how you've changed, the more he sees that you're devoted, the easier it will be for him to get there. Patience is key."

Talking to Laura brings back all those years I waffled in impatience. But now I know there is so much blessing ahead if she just stays the course.

Cheryl
1994–1997

The question I asked God in spring of 1994—*what next?*—characterized my life for the next three years.

Jeff and I settled into a comfortable place of managing the kids together and parenting them the best we knew how for the situation we were in. We got along and treated each other with respect in order to make it all work. At least the girls had the advantage of both parents heavily involved in their lives. I managed a few smiles, and so did he. A little healing was taking place. I kept up the habit of daily time with God, praying about many things, including the renewal of my marriage. But to no avail. Jeff treated me with unbelievable kindness, while showing no interest in us as a couple.

Every time I saw Jeff, I was reminded of my sin and the brokenness of our family. The fracture never seemed to heal. It only became wider. He and I never talked about it. It was like it had been thrown under the rug to be forgotten.

My desire for restoration began to wane. I was exhausted. I was frustrated with God because, once again, I doubted what I thought he had whispered to me. It seemed a far-fetched dream that I must have made up out of my own guilt and selfish desires. I cried myself to sleep countless nights. I felt like God was punishing me. I wrote pages and pages of prayers in my journals, begging God to answer my request.

One day I couldn't take it anymore and decided to "move on" with my life. I told myself I was giving up the dream of a second chance with Jeff. He had been dating other women, and I started dating other people too. Then God brought me back, reminding me of the journey I'd committed to. For three years, I would repeat this cycle numerous times.

Divorced people would often tell me that after time had elapsed, we would all get used to the *way it was.* The girls would get used to being shuttled back and forth between homes week in and week out. Christmas morning would someday be fine with one parent missing, and vacations would be fun again. But a couple of years into the divorce, the sting was still there. I believed deep in my heart that our being apart was not God's plan, and I still held out hope for remarriage.

Sometimes it was confusing for me, because I knew people who were divorced and appeared to be experiencing renewed lives. They felt peace about their situation and *seemed* to have God's blessing. Why, then, did I not feel the same? I came to the conclusion that everyone's situation was different, and for whatever reason, God was calling me to a different path. My path seemed harder! But I was to learn that God was teaching something that was eminently worth any amount of struggle. I would come to question whether God *ever* excused divorce.

I loved Jesus and desired to follow him with all I had in me. I also loved my husband, the man I had divorced, and it dawned on me that by following the Lord and loving Jeff without any expectation of anything in return, I was beginning to love Jeff more than I ever had before. I cried out to God in prayer and begged him to open Jeff's heart to me again.

Every now and then, I mentioned to Jeff why I thought we should try again, and every time he shut me down or ignored me. I wanted to believe that God was moving in his heart, but I had no evidence. I was wearing myself out getting up every day at five o'clock, dropping into my chair, and giving it all up again. Some days I tried to journal but had no energy to write. Occasionally I just sat there and cried, but more often, I was crying on the inside. I had a constant ache in my soul that was so overwhelming, it was a physical sensation. The pain was all about my regrets—that I'd hurt Jeff and the girls, that I'd disappointed God by my lack of obedience. I was sometimes consumed with anger at myself for having been so selfish, stubborn, and hardhearted. And I felt powerless to fix all these things.

One day as I sat in my chair, an amazing peace came over me. I heard the voice once again. *Cheryl, don't give up. I have a plan, and I need you to stick with me. I'm working behind the scenes where you can't see. Trust me. Most people do not wait long enough on me. I am molding and shaping you, and I am molding and shaping Jeff. My timing is perfect, you'll see.*

Well, that was all well and good and sounded perfectly nice. But I wasn't feeling nice. I shouted back to God that I didn't know if I could go on. I told him I was exhausted and wanted to quit. Patience is definitely not a virtue of mine! Again, I received the reminder that this journey was not about me, but about him. I was still years away from understanding what it meant every time God sent me the message that this was *all about him.*

More and more frequently, when I went to God with a "what about me?" plea, it was as if he handed me a camera lens to look through. The lens was one that could be adjusted to focus either on the foreground or the background, and I'd see the picture change right before my eyes. When a situation that I'd seen as "all about me" shifted slightly, I'd suddenly see God in the picture, front and center, while I remained in the background, a little blurry. Through a word of Scripture or words he spoke directly to me in my journaling times, God kept handing me this lens. The sad thing was how quickly I handed it back to him! It took a long time before I was able to maintain this new way of seeing in my daily life, rather than glimpsing it in occasional moments. The focus needed to be on God, not me.

Where was Jeff in the picture I saw through that magic lens? He was there too, yet it was always clear that a picture of "Jeff and me" was secondary to the picture of "God and me." I sometimes wondered about the picture of "Jeff and God," but it wasn't my business to know about that at the time.

Even though I was seeking God daily, I was still living in the world. I was single, and I met men in various places, but I didn't go on many dates. When I did, I kept it casual and told myself it was harmless. After all, I wanted to keep my feelers out *just in case* nothing ever materialized between Jeff and me.

Still, everywhere I turned, the thought of reconciliation hit me in the face. Families in restaurants, single parents playing dad *and* mom, kids abandoned, and couples facing the unbearable pain of separation. These were constant reminders of how desperately I wanted my marriage back. I wanted my family back.

My friends were my lifeline. We had endless hours of conversations about my path, my conviction about what God was telling me, and the probability of it ever working out the way I wanted it to. They stuck by me, but it was hard on them. They loved me and didn't want to see me hurt any more than I already was. They often encouraged me to "move on," which meant I should let go of my crazy idea and try to find someone new. But there was something deep in me, something I didn't really understand, that made me keep listening to the ways God was speaking to me. This was so hard! How do you tell your friends that their advice was wonderful and well meaning but that you've decided to ignore it in favor of this "voice" you hear every morning in your journal time? Much of the time I felt like it was just "me and God" because I had to stop listening to all the conflicting advice from others.

Still, there were days I did not want to pray. At times I questioned why I even cared about putting my marriage back together. It was when these mind games and distorted thoughts took over that God came crashing in and reminded me of the assignment he'd given me. I have to be honest— I gave up praying many times during these years. I was exhausted from the waiting.

But the one thing I could count on was the arms of Jesus gently coming around me. Countless times he pulled me back, and I was able to recover my focus. I still had a hard time keeping hope alive, because nothing on planet Earth seemed to offer hope for Jeff and me.

One morning, as I stood in my kitchen waiting for my coffee to brew, I thought about what I'd do next. I looked at my chair, with the journals, pens, and Bible beside it. But I just couldn't do it. I decided to pick up the newspaper instead and sat down at the dining-room table. I read the articles, but I was distracted the whole time. I kept feeling as though I was being called to my chair. It was so strong it was almost like a phone ringing in my ear. No matter how much you don't want to talk to anyone, the ringing eventually compels you to answer just to make it stop. I finally threw down the newspaper and went to my chair. Too stubborn to pray, I began reading Psalms. Sure enough, before long I was having a conversation with God. Somehow he always wins!

Around four years after the divorce, I started getting some tiny glimpses of hope, but they always seemed to be immediately dashed. Jeff would drop the girls off after a T-ball game, and I'd ask him to stay for dinner. He had always said no whenever I asked him to spend any time with me, but for some reason, he started to say yes once in a while. It seemed as if we were getting more comfortable together, but then he would abruptly leave with barely a good-bye, like he was angry. Sometimes I'd ask him to stay and he'd say no. It confused me.

Because of my upbeat nature and outgoing personality, most people would never have recognized that I was distraught. My close friends knew, but for others I put a smile on my face, did things energetically, and pretended that life was great. There was no point putting my pain out there for the world to see. My life was busy, and I was always around people. I was heavily involved in church, going to Bible study, worship, Wednesday night services, and everything else. But my kids were my focus. They were in elementary school, so most of my life revolved around them. I always picked them up from school, and whenever they were not with Jeff, I spent time actively doing things with them. So for the sake of the kids, and to preserve some dignity, I managed to appear fairly happy most of the time.

It was nearly five years into the divorce. I sat restlessly in my usual seat at Starbucks near my house. People shuffled in and out pursuing their daily caffeine addictions. I'd gotten in the habit of coming here with my journal or my laptop, and for some reason the atmosphere comforted me. It wasn't unusual for me to get into light conversations with people, but on this day I recognized one handsome man at a nearby table, and a familiar temptation popped up.

It's just harmless conversation…

To give you the context, the previous evening, Jeff had stayed for din-ner with the girls and me. We were having a nice time, joking and laugh-ing, and I couldn't help picturing us as the family we were always meant to be. After everyone had finished eating, I thought I'd try to extend the fun.

"Anyone up for a board game?"

"Yeah!" the girls chimed in and ran off to pick one. Jeff followed them into the other room, and soon I heard choruses of "No, Daddy, please stay." I could hear his low voice and soon the girls seemed happy again. I don't know what Jeff promised them, but they all came back, the girls hanging on Jeff's arms, and headed for the front door. He glanced in my direction.

"See you later. Let's talk tomorrow about my business trip next week."

I followed them toward the door. "Girls, would you run and start your baths?" After lots more hugs and kisses for Jeff, they ran off.

"Do you have to leave? What's so important that you can't just stay a little bit?"

Jeff opened the door and stepped out on the porch.

"Cheryl, let's not go there again, okay? I'm not trying to be rude. I just need to go. I'll talk to you tomorrow."

He turned and walked to his car without a backward glance. I felt like I was at the end of my rope with Jeff. He was friendly enough and tried hard not to hurt my feelings, but that was all. I was out of patience.

As I mentioned, patience wasn't a virtue of mine. I was always some-one who could barely wait sixty seconds to warm up my leftovers in the microwave. I was being asked to continue being patient, even though I'd already been holding out for five years.

God—you're kidding me, right? I gotta tell you, it's not that funny.

Instant results—that's what I wanted. I'd presumed that once I was willing to make this huge commitment—breaking it off with Todd, believing God for the repair of my marriage—then he would quickly come through with results. And in my timing, of course.

So sitting in that coffee shop, I was thinking how long it had been going on. And after all this time, it wasn't even going anywhere. A sickening feeling came over me. *It could even go on a lot longer than this*, I thought. How could I possibly keep this up?

So rewind to where I looked up from my journal and saw this man I recognized at the next table. He looked up at the same time and smiled. I nodded. We were both regulars, and we'd exchanged similar acknowledgements with each other many times. I noticed he didn't wear a wedding ring.

Maybe it was time for me to speak up. Maybe I needed to take things into my own hands.

I looked back at my journal. *No. God knows what he's doing.* He was telling me, over and over, to hold out for reconciliation of my marriage. And he was giving me just enough faith for a single day. Each morsel of hope was just enough to carry me to the next. If my faith waned—like in this moment facing this handsome man—the likelihood of me abandoning ship and not hanging on was enormous.

I needed to hang on. I refocused my attention on my journal and started writing.

"What if I'm reading this all wrong?" I wrote. "Maybe I'm misunderstanding God. There's a good possibility he won't choose to heal my marriage, even after my obedience. What am I supposed to do with that? Is all I can do to keep praying? If he chooses not to restore us, I can only trust that he'll let me know. In the meantime, I just have to persist in faith and prayer.

"This has been an incredible journey God's been taking me on. The last few years have been so heavy with regret, and the learning curve has been steep. But all those mornings wrestling with God have taught me a few things. I can review them in my mind and continue to write them here to remind myself of how far I've come."

With my favorite blue pen, I scribbled, "I've taken responsibility for making the wrong choices and having wrong attitudes. My mistakes began way back in the early days of our marriage, when I consistently chose not to speak openly with Jeff about the depths of my heart."

My pen hovered over the page before continuing. "I've learned that it wasn't just Jeff's fault that he didn't see me. I was the one who created the situation that kept distance between us and lowered my defenses."

For a long time, I'd held on to the idea that Jeff had been the major cause of my discontent. Every time I'd become aware of another failure of mine, I'd immediately jump to, "But Jeff did this" or "Jeff did that." In my mind, he made me do what I did.

I began writing again. "I've quit the blame game. I've learned to confront the truth. Despite the pain and anger within me, I know I have to face my own responsibility for the place I was in. This is evidence of my growth."

I put down the pen again and resisted the urge to glance again at the man nearby. Since I'd begun pursuing a relationship with God, I'd been plagued by this concept of obedience. *Ick. What a word. Like a child forced to submit to Dad's authority.*

I scrawled the word out with a different colored pen. "Obedience."

It's embarrassing to admit that I'd had to learn that obedience to God, to marriage vows—and to all the usual moral guidelines—was essential for grownups. I was always given a choice whether to obey or not. Often I'd chosen to willfully disobey what I knew was right, initially because of the ache in my heart, though I was the one who had left it unattended. That was one of the biggest lessons I'd learned. I had to be open and honest about what was in my heart, or I'd sink into despair yet again.

To see the truth of my foolish choices written out was humiliating. There were plenty of physical and mental warning signs every time I was about to make such a choice—a dull ache in my stomach, a constant nervous feeling. I sometimes felt fear. And as I continued to walk the wrong path, my soul felt torn into shreds. Trying to escape the lack of peace became an obsession, just like the disobedience was.

I thought back to the time I flew to California to visit Todd. As I sat on the plane, I leaned my head against the window, watching the clouds go by, and tried to identify the source of the fear that seemed to be lodged in my stomach. I was so excited to spend time with Todd; yet I kept thinking, *What if the plane crashes?* I was obsessed with the thought that somehow, something would go wrong, and not only would Jeff find out about the affair, but the girls would be left motherless. All because of my own selfishness. I spent the entire flight battling my thoughts and even considered immediately flying home once we arrived at the airport in California. I had a choice; I could have done that. But the minute I got off the plane and found Todd waiting for me in the airport, I pushed those thoughts away and let the "high" of being with Todd overshadow every rational thought. I never felt peace, yet I kept making the wrong choices.

So why did I choose to continue in disobedience? Why did I allow myself to self-destruct? As I pondered, the answer surfaced: selfishness. Plain and simple, "I want what I want when I want it," and I chose to ignore the destructive aspects of my behavior.

Even during the past few years when I'd been trying to follow the Lord, I sometimes made choices that I didn't believe were God's plan for me—like staying with Todd way too long. I yearned to follow God but continued to allow myself to be misled. Sometimes I could not withstand the temptation and would go out with other men, and because I had a hard time keeping my sexual desire at bay, I would put myself in compromising situations and go too far. I wanted to feel desired. Wanted. And I knew I could get a quick fix of self-esteem by being attractive to someone.

"I haven't been fully committed to God," I wrote. "I didn't want to do it his way and sometimes I crossed the line purposefully. It led nowhere but to more confusion. Instead of peace, I only experienced greater turmoil."

Then I wrote a final line: "Consider your level of commitment to God." At that moment, I looked up and noticed an older woman walking by, carrying a Bible and a cup of coffee. She settled herself at a table near me. For some reason I felt like she could see right through me. I averted my eyes, filled with shame. It felt as though she could see what a horrible person I'd been.

I set my journal aside and opened my Bible. I read, "Therefore, there is now no condemnation for those who are in Christ Jesus" (Romans 8:1). I let those words sink in for a moment and something else came to my mind. *Hadn't there been many times when I chose obedience, even though it wasn't what I wanted? Wasn't that a step in the right direction?*

Much of the time I was faithfully holding out for reconciliation with Jeff, I honestly didn't want it. I was tired of the whole thing. I would rather have been out dating and finding a new Mr. Right. But the peace I felt from stepping out in obedience was worth it.

There had been one guy, Rick, who I'd been friendly with. We went on a few dates, but eventually, it started to feel wrong. One night, he called to ask me out for Saturday. I recall thinking, *Now's my chance to follow what God's telling me.*

"Um, you know, Rick, I don't think so." I cringed as I said it. In truth, I would have enjoyed going out with him again.

"Okay," Rick said. "Well, how about Sunday?"

"The thing is… I don't think I'm ready for this. Dating, I mean." This was hard! I hated to hurt people's feelings. And I really did like Rick's company. "It's not you at all. I like hanging out with you. It's just…"

"It's okay, Cheryl. I understand. It's hard being divorced."

I was shocked. Wow! It seemed God was making this easy for me.

"Yes, it's hard. But…well, I'm sure I'll see you at church sometime."

After we hung up, I felt a sense of peace filling my spirit, and it truly was beyond understanding. I wondered if I was gradually getting to a place where I wanted to please God more than men, more than myself. God had given me the strength to "just say no," and I was amazed. It was a huge change, one I never fully considered before, and it felt great. God was truly working in me, changing me from the inside out.

As I sat there in the coffee shop reliving this scene in my mind, I was once again wrestling with an obedience issue. I'd gained so much insight already. So why was I still tempted to disobey what I thought God was telling me? Why did that guy sitting across from me look so appealing?

Selfishness? Could it really all come down to that? I knew my self-focus had been a problem all along. I wasn't able to see beyond my own needs and desires. I believed *I* needed a more fulfilling marriage and so *I* needed to end the emptiness. Had I ever given much thought to how I was hurting the girls or ruining Jeff's life? When thoughts like that came up, I only rationalized them away. And right now, *I* needed a man's attention because *I* was tired of being rejected by Jeff. Just thinking about walking up to this guy and saying hello seemed like such a simple, innocent thing.

But what was the real harm?

I wanted to get up and get a refill. Maybe a muffin too. But could I walk past this handsome man and not do anything?

Maybe I should wait. Once again, I refocused my attention to my journal and that last line I'd written.

It was painful to recall how selfish I was. As I thought about it, I realized I'd been deceived, too. I bought into the lies our culture tells us. I had assumptions about life and marriage, and it never occurred to me to question them. I believed that once I fell in love and married, all would be conquered. I'd be set for life—no more problems. What a lie.

"Lie number one," I wrote. "Marriage equals happiness."

I thought I deserved to be happy. Doesn't the world owe me that one thing—simple happiness? What a shock to find that marriage didn't provide instant happiness. When I emerged from the wedding fog and realized my husband was not perfect, I began to entertain the thought that I married the wrong person, and the obvious answer was to go find the right one.

Compounding all of this was the idea that I wasn't the kind of person who would *ever* have an affair.

"Lie number two: I'm not that kind of person," I wrote next.

Most of us believe that about ourselves. If I'd at least acknowledged the possibility that I *could* have an affair—especially if I'd recognized my vulnerability—I could have protected myself. No one is completely safe and immune from falling into sin. I believed a little flirting with men was harmless. But I found out the truth.

As my mind flitted across the many harmful lies I bought into, I had to face the biggest one I *chose* to believe—and yes, it was a choice.

"The kids would be fine." I wrote that down as lie number three, and underlined it several times.

I desperately needed to trust that this was true. That no matter what I did, the kids were resilient; they wouldn't suffer; they'd adjust. I found out that this was only partly the case. Since Jeff and I each devoted our full selves to the girls and totally cooperated where they were concerned, never speaking an ill word against each other, our daughters weathered it fairly well. But I couldn't kid myself. They did suffer. That morning Brittany had given me an extra hug and asked, "Are you okay, Mom?" She was just in elementary school, but always so concerned about me and Jeff. And last night when Jeff had dropped the girls off with me, Lauren had clung extra hard to her daddy, not wanting to let him go. The girls wanted their family together. They dreamed of it and prayed for it.

So the idea that our divorce wouldn't hurt the kids was one of the most destructive lies that deceived me. Thank God, I was starting to see through all the deception. And I was beginning to learn the truths that replaced them.

As I sat making my little list and coming face to face with all my mistakes, I still felt helpless to fix my situation. I wanted reconciliation, and Jeff didn't. End of story. I was powerless. I figured God must have put me in this situation on purpose. He didn't want me taking the credit for anything he was doing. I had to be in a place of total dependency, complete surrender, before God could work with me.

There was such an interesting interplay between choice, obedience, and surrender. I had to obey; I had to continually choose properly. But I also had to lay myself open to God. I had to admit I could not walk this path by myself. Breaking off the relationship with Todd was so difficult that I never would have been able to do it on my own. It was a God-sized job, and he couldn't do his work until I let go of my self-sufficiency and let him work. "Let go and let God." I hated those pithy bumper stickers. But the words turned out to be a profound truth.

One of the most difficult things I'd learned was that, no matter how much I desired reconciliation in my marriage, no matter how much I desired to follow God's plan, God wanted me to desire something else more.

He wanted me to desire him.

I had been journaling in my chair a few days before, asking God,

"What do you want me to do? I am following you, trying to follow your plan, trying to pursue reconciliation with Jeff, but nothing's changing. What's going on?"

What I wrote next was a question that sounded like it was being whispered in my ear.

"What do you want the most, Cheryl?"

An easy one. "I want to restore my family."

"And what if that never happens?"

I stopped writing and fought the gut reaction of anger and frustration. I thought carefully before writing, "I want to follow your plan for me, whatever it is."

The next thing I heard was mind boggling. "And what if it's not about the plan, Cheryl? What if it's about something else?"

I didn't know what that meant. I threw myself back in my chair, and let go of my pen, wanting to give up. "Well, *what* then?" I nearly yelled. *What is this about?*

Slowly, like thawing ice, it dawned on me. I needed to desire *God himself* before I could truly desire his best for my marriage.

Wow. That was a tough one. How much did I desire God? I began to pray that I would *desire* to desire God. I gained the understanding that God would not work on my relationship with Jeff until I allowed him to work on my relationship with *him*.

This led me to one of the most profound realizations of all—that all of my problems with my marriage were much more about *me and God* than about me and Jeff. All those mornings sitting in my chair? They were for the purpose of getting to know God and letting him mold me. I had to admit, my chair had taken on a new look over the years. It was now perfectly shaped for me. And I realized that my chair represented the molding God was doing in my soul. He was shaping me into what he wanted me to be, not necessarily what I wanted or thought I should be. I was being re-created. In his image.

Sitting in the coffee shop and pondering all of this, I put my pen down once again. I was ready for that second cup of coffee. I grabbed my purse and started toward the counter. The man at the next table looked up, smiled, and seemed about to say something. I gave him a polite smile and kept on walking.

NINE

Jeff
1994–1997

Survival mode. That's how I spent those next few years. My life was my work, my kids, and the boys at the church youth group. When I had Brittany and Lauren with me, I was so happy. When I didn't, I poured myself into the lives of the kids at church. And when I wasn't doing that, I was at the gym working out. I was trying to keep myself healthy, physically and spiritually. I didn't know what else to do.

Life was always complicated. Cheryl and I never fought, but we had to be in contact all the time. Our schedule required us to cart the girls here and there, attending games, taking them to birthday parties, sleepovers, and everything else they were involved in. As the girls got older, they were more and more clever about trying to get Cheryl and me together. There would be a meeting at school and the girls would ask me, "You're both going, right?" Cheryl and I both went but in separate cars. Sometimes we drove together to school or a T-ball game, and that was uncomfortable. For the longest time, I couldn't look Cheryl in the eye.

I was definitely playing the victim role. I was the innocent bystander wounded by Cheryl's selfish actions. She had declared war on our marriage, and I was a casualty. My suffering did not abate as my mind continued to seethe with blame. My anger hung on, or maybe *I* hung on to *it*.

I dated a little here and there. A couple of times I began relationships, but they only lasted a few months each. I started to think about marrying one of these women and what it would be like with the kids, and that made me back off. I couldn't explain it—it just didn't seem right. I was still a couple of years away from believing Cheryl and I could possibly put it back together, so that wasn't it. The truth was I couldn't imagine anyone else even trying to be a mom to the girls. And I couldn't imagine myself with one of these women permanently in my life. I *already* had a wife—the thought of looking for another was too surreal. I was lonely and needed companionship but never felt like getting serious with any of the women I dated.

The older the girls got, the more I saw Cheryl because the kids had more activities and we both wanted to be involved in everything. Since the girls didn't want this divorce—it wasn't their fault—I did everything I could to make it as comfortable as possible for them. I tried to make the best of a bad situation. They were first in my life. If they needed me, I'd drop everything and be there. As angry and uneasy as I was with Cheryl, I had to admit she put the girls first too.

When she wrote that letter and told me she'd become a Christian, it seemed so unlikely. With true believers, you see their belief in the way they live their lives, and I just didn't see that with her. What impacted me over time was that, when I went over to her house, she had her Bible out, verses written on scraps of paper all over the place, and her journals lying around. I couldn't imagine it was all some kind of show. Maybe she *was* being changed.

Eventually I started noticing a change of heart. In everything she did, the way she lived her life, she seemed more peaceful and confident. She treated me so sweetly, and she seemed to care more about people than I'd ever seen before. Her relationships with her friends seemed deeper and more real. She was more passionate about life at a deeper level. I noticed the subtle changes, and I wondered whether God was working on her heart. This wasn't a foreign concept to me. I'd been going to church and attending Bible study, so I knew it was possible for someone to be changed by Jesus. It was just strange to think it could happen to Cheryl after all the torture she'd put me through.

At the same time, God was slowly, almost imperceptibly, changing me too. The anger was fading, bit by bit. It didn't seem to be from anything I was doing, since I didn't have a clue how to change myself. I'd been on a spiritual journey of my own, and I thought maybe God was starting to heal my heart.

Gradually I started thawing toward Cheryl. Sometime around the fifth year after the divorce, I came to pick up the girls and she asked me to stay for dinner. When that first happened, I didn't want to have dinner with her. I didn't want to spend *any* time with her. But I had just begun to have some sincere realizations of my own failings in the marriage. I was in a men's Bible study and was learning about God's plan for marriage, and it occurred to me that I had failed miserably as a husband. Maybe this whole disastrous situation wasn't all Cheryl's fault after all.

So one of the times she asked me to stay for dinner, I finally said yes. We slowly started getting comfortable with each other again. But sometimes it just freaked me out to be there, and I'd have this swell of anger and have to leave. I know it confused her tremendously.

Some days I could be around her, other days I couldn't stand it. I was scared because I saw the changes in her and began to understand they were real. That put me in the driver's seat. It was up to me—if I said the word, we could put this thing back together. But that petrified me. How could I trust her? How did I know I wasn't going to go through hell and back all over again?

When Cheryl read me that letter back in 1993, my reaction was furious and instantaneous. I was never proud of my response. I wished I could have been sensitive enough to listen to her with an open heart, an open mind, but I was so angry at her. I couldn't take any more.

But the cool thing was that I kept the letter. Even though I didn't want to hear it, I probably read it a dozen times over the next several months. And every time I read it, I cried. There was something important about having that piece of paper. When she came to me, I wasn't ready to hear it—it wasn't the right time for me. But I had the letter, and when it was a better time, when I could actually think about and comprehend what she was saying, I was in a better frame of mind. Eventually I took to heart what she had written.

Still, how does a guy get beyond the kind of betrayal and agony Cheryl put me through? I knew I had to forgive her, but I had no idea how. There were a few people around me who knew the whole story, and some of them couldn't wrap their minds around the possibility of forgiveness. They were Christians, but they cared about me, and they were human. They would never have recommended taking Cheryl back, even if they believed in it because it was biblical. The messages were conflicting, and I found myself constantly in torment over what to do.

At the same time, I was working with the kids at church and seeing the results of families getting divorced. Some of the kids were miserable. I kept thinking, *If I had the power to change this situation for my girls, would I do it?*

Cheryl wrote me another letter about four years into being divorced. It was even more powerful than the first one. She explained, again, the work God was doing in her life. She confessed that she had been wrong and behaved wrongly in our marriage. And she challenged me to seriously seek

God's will for us. She was logical too, asking me, "What's the worst that can happen?" If we tried reconciliation and it didn't work, we'd simply end up in the same place. But if it did work... She painted a picture of the happy family life we'd both always dreamed of.

One part of Cheryl's letter was particularly compelling. She wrote that her friend Marci had told her, "Tell Jeff what's on your mind and heart, because if you die tomorrow, I don't want to be the one at your funeral telling him how much you loved him!"

Cheryl truly believed we were meant to be together.

I didn't want to, but I started praying about it. After a while I felt my resentment softening. But then I'd think, *This is too weird; how can I consider getting back together with this person who ripped my heart out? Tore up my family? What am I going to tell my mom and dad, my sister, my brothers, my friends—everybody who went through this mess with me?*

I started seeing new things. I was teaching the high school boys a study on the disciplines of a godly man, and I realized I was *not* that guy when I was married. I wasn't a godly husband, and I wasn't a spiritual leader. There wasn't any spirituality in the marriage at all. I learned about the emotional connection Cheryl missed in our marriage. I completely didn't get it—it just never came naturally to me to sit down and talk to my wife, to listen to her, listen to her heart, and also explain what was going on inside me. I didn't know how to connect at a deeper level.

When we were married, I never focused on anything deeper than the next bike ride on the beach or where we were going for dinner. I worked hard at making money, which came naturally to me. My life was about "fun" and "stuff" and "hanging out." No wonder Cheryl felt lonely. She must have looked at me and thought, *The lights are on, but nobody's home.* I wasn't there for her in the way she needed me.

Thinking back, I realized that if somebody had spoken to me about "connecting" with my wife or listening to her, I would have brushed it off. I'd have said, "Of course I connect with my wife! Of course I listen to her!" I was clueless about the levels of depth that were possible, even necessary, in a marriage. Nobody ever talked about those things—at least, guys never did. Men are supposed to be strong and reserved; if we get too emotional, it's a sign of weakness. Nobody teaches us the truth: that taking the risk to go deeper emotionally, to truly *know* somebody and *be known*, is one of the greatest ways to find fulfillment in this life.

As I came to this awareness, it frustrated and angered me that I'd been so ignorant. Why didn't I know how to be a godly husband? I was raised in the church, so why didn't I know what a God-centered relationship looked like? I was also mad at myself. Why had I walked away from all things spiritual? I knew better. If I'd made the right choices in college, none of this mess would have happened. It was becoming increasingly clear that I bore a lot of responsibility for the way things went.

So there was some lingering resentment—toward the church and toward myself—at the same time that I was drawing closer to the Lord. For the first time in my life, I understood the difference between being a Christian who does the "religious" thing and having a relationship with Jesus. I was getting the relationship part. I understood more about how much God loved me and how much he'd given me over the years, and I wanted to be obedient to him.

Surrender was a daily thing. Every day I woke up and prayed, *God, I want to walk with you today. Show me how to do it.*

I finally had a turning point. I lay in my bed, and Proverbs 3:5–6, which I had memorized as a little boy, came to me. It says, "Trust in the LORD with all your heart and lean not on your own understanding; in all your ways acknowledge him, and he will make your paths straight." I realized I did everything in my own understanding instead of leaning on God.

I wasn't trusting him; I was trying to understand this whole situation with Cheryl on my own terms. That realization was huge for me, and I knew it, even as it came to me.

I didn't want to do this. I didn't want to think about whether Cheryl might be right, whether I should consider what she was saying. But I'd been carrying the anger for years, and it was beating me up. My being mad wasn't doing anything to her, but it was eating me alive. It affected everything—my relationships, my work.

This is stupid. The futility of my ongoing bitterness struck me head-on. I had to let it go. I knew I was to the point I could finally forgive her. I was nowhere near thinking about getting back together. But after I began to forgive Cheryl, I could pick up the girls and actually look at her without hatred eating a hole inside me.

It wasn't anything I did. On my own, I might have carried the anger forever. I didn't know how to make it go away, and I still don't. That was God showing me that his ways are higher than my ways. I never understood that. He did it, not me.

I was slowly forgiving Cheryl and letting go of the pain and anger from the past. With this new frame of mind, God prepared me for the next steps in our journey. If I hadn't lived it, I'd have never believed it.

TEN

Cheryl
1997

Around Brittany and Lauren's eighth birthday, I was sitting in the bleachers on a hot summer afternoon watching their team play softball, chatting with some of the other parents around me. Looking out over the field, I happened to catch the eye of the opposing team's coach. His gaze lingered. Weird. I looked away.

Later in the game a parent from the other team came over and asked if I was married—the coach wanted to know. I struggled with my answer. Obviously the answer was no, but my gut told me it wasn't that simple. I quickly thought of the long road I'd already walked, hoping to rekindle my marriage, and the number of times I'd dated other men and then felt bad because I wasn't being obedient. This was a test.

But I was going to fail this one. I ignored what my heart told me and once again determined to go my own way. I let the coach know I was single. After the game he found me, and we walked to the parking lot, talking. He asked me on a date for the next day, and I was excited. I yearned for companionship and the thrill of romance. Yet my stomach was in knots. I couldn't even pray the next morning. I couldn't face God while I was blatantly snubbing him.

I ignored the uncomfortable feeling and went on the date anyway. I immediately fell head over heels for this stranger and began to bless God for bringing this wonderful man into my life. I *just knew* he was the man God meant as my reward after I'd diligently sacrificed in hopes of mending my marriage. The next three weeks were intense. I saw this man every single day—we were obsessed with each other. Immediately I was convinced that marriage was inevitable and my future was with him. I tried to forget about pursuing Jeff and pushed him into the category of *ex-husband*. Jeff was also dating someone, so I convinced myself this was God's plan. I was sure we would never get back together and was at peace with it.

Then the bottom dropped out. One day, this guy didn't call. And he never called again. I had no idea what happened or why. I was crushed and didn't understand. He never explained. I felt like I had nowhere to turn.

I ran desperately back to God. I had to go "back" to him because I had left him—my first love—for three weeks. I was humiliated at how easily I could fall away. How effortlessly I could be deceived—again—after all I'd learned.

It brought me to my knees. I asked forgiveness for running away. But I had to be honest with God. I had tasted what it might be like to have a man in my life again and to be in love. That was what I wanted.

In a quiet moment one morning in my chair, Jesus—not a man but God—wrapped his arms around me and lovingly urged me to get back in the game of reconciliation. I admitted for the millionth time that I did not know if I could keep going with this journey.

I sat awhile in despair. Will I always be such a failure at following God? Will I ever get it right? And what if he keeps dragging it out forever—can I stand it? For some reason, I opened my Bible and turned to the book of Deuteronomy, chapter 8. Here is a portion of what I read:

> Be careful to obey all the commands I am giving you today. Then
> you will live and multiply, and you will enter and occupy the land

the LORD swore to give your ancestors. Remember how the LORD your God led you through the wilderness for these forty years, humbling you and testing you to prove your character, and to find out whether or not you would obey his commands... He did it to teach you that people do not live by bread alone; rather, we live by every word that comes from the mouth of the LORD... Think about it: Just as a parent disciplines a child, the LORD your God disciplines you for your own good.

So obey the commands of the LORD your God by walking in his ways and fearing him. For the LORD your God is bringing you into a good land of flowing streams and pools of water, with fountains and springs that gush out in the valleys and hills... It is a land where food is plentiful and nothing is lacking... When you have eaten your fill, be sure to praise the LORD your God for the good land he has given you. (verses 1–3, 5–7, 9–10, NLT)

I sat stunned. Breathless. Numb. I realized that for the last few years since I'd come to know Jesus, I always held something back. I always kept in the back of my mind the "right" to make my own choices, determine my own life. God had already blessed me so much by being patient with me and not allowing Jeff or me to marry someone else—very unusual for people in our situation. I felt God telling me that he would restore this thing if I would just *obey his commands*. He had promised to bring me into a good land. Was I going to let him?

Part of the deal was that he required I not date anyone. I was to focus solely on obeying his Word and love Jeff unconditionally, no matter how he acted toward me. Although previously I'd had inklings that I shouldn't date, this was the first time it was made perfectly clear to me in my prayer time. No other men. Period.

My initial reaction was a big fat NO! I am not sacrificing my life for something I do not have a guarantee on. After all, I am getting older and want to enjoy what life I have left. I told God I didn't think I could do it. He didn't respond. He didn't have to.

I got up the next morning to read my Bible and pray. I was extremely distracted. I couldn't concentrate on one word I read and had trouble writing anything down in my journal. I stared into space. This went on for two entire weeks. Eventually I was exhausted. My own stubbornness and pride were wearing me out. I needed to humble myself and give up control. When I finally said, "Okay God, I give up. I am at the end of myself," I felt his peace and presence once again. How could he still keep coming back to me, when I was such a loser at following him? I had never felt more loved in my life. Once again, I surrendered, but this time it felt different. It may have been the first time I actually meant it. I told God I would obey. And I felt peace.

Almost immediately I noticed a difference in Jeff's demeanor. He seemed calm and noticeably interested in what was going on in my life. I was reluctant to think this was anything more than a phase. It seemed too strange, and I didn't trust it. Of course, it was exactly what I'd prayed for, yet I still didn't trust it! I pinched myself, thinking this could be the blessing God had promised me. I had written Jeff a second letter, asking him to seriously consider reconciliation. Jeff never acknowledged receiving the letter, and it was a grueling couple of months, wondering what he might be thinking. But it was encouraging to see that I didn't go ballistic with impatience.

Every time I was tempted to say something about the letter, I held myself back and immediately sought the Lord. It was one of the hardest things I had to do, but somehow I prevailed. Was God really building patience in me?

Finally I felt it would be okay to call Jeff.

"Hi, Cheryl."

"Jeff, I need to talk to you."

Long pause. Then, "Yes, I got the letter."

Of course he knew what I was thinking. We rarely spoke about anything but the girls, and it was probably obvious from my tone of voice.

Jeff continued. "Listen, Cheryl. I appreciate it—really. I've come a long way. Everything you wrote in the letter…it was good. And you're right, we need to try and follow God's plan. The past is in the past, but I just don't think I can ever consider getting back together."

I couldn't even respond, so he went on, "We're doing great, handling the kids and seeing each other all the time. Don't you think so?"

"Um. Yeah."

"But I think it's time for you to give up this idea and move on with your life. I don't sense the same calling or direction that you do. I've got to follow what I think God is telling *me*. And I just don't think reconciliation is the answer."

I felt like someone punched me in the stomach. Again I doubted my God and what he had promised me. Worse than that, Jeff's rejection filled me with such a gut-wrenching pain that I realized once and for all that *I really loved him.* My love for Jeff was something bigger than me, not based on romance or expectations or shared dreams. It was God's love.

But I couldn't tell Jeff that. I don't know how we ended that conversation, but we hung up quickly. And the next thing I thought I heard God say was that he was going to get Jeff's attention.

Really, God? How? I want to trust you, but I don't know if I'm even hearing you clearly.

I flashed on Mark 9:24. "I do believe; help me overcome my unbelief!" Would this roller coaster never end?

My best friend, Halle, and I walked through the park, discussing what was going on in our lives. She'd been with me through the divorce and all the ups and downs of the past several years, and sometimes I worried I was wearing her out. She had to be tired of it by now—even I was tired of it! But she always hung in there with me. When I told her of Jeff's latest rejection, she was silent.

"Halle?" I prompted.

"Sweetie, I don't know how to say this."

That was unusual for Halle; she was always one to shoot straight from the hip. "Just tell me," I told her.

"I know you're doing your best to follow God's leading. And you're being so faithful—really, I'm so proud of you. Your faith has been amazing. I've learned so much just from watching you. And to think, just a few years ago, you'd never even read the Bible. It's unbelievable."

"But...?" I prompted.

"But I think there comes a point when you have to look at reality. I hate to see you holding your life up this way. I don't think Jeff is ever going to come around. You can't spend the rest of your life beating your head against a brick wall."

"You're saying I should give up?"

"It's not *giving up*...it's facing the truth. It's acting based on what you *know* to be true. And what you know is that you've given this more than enough time. I don't think it's going to happen. Maybe you and Jeff aren't meant to get back together."

"What about what God seems to be telling me? You're saying I'm not understanding him correctly?"

"I'm saying it's possible to mistake your own deep desire for a message from God."

Ouch. That one got me. Could I be attributing my own desires to God?

I spent a few days thinking about that one, praying about it, and considering whether Halle could be right. I had all these journals where I'd recorded my ongoing dialogue with God. Did I make it all up? Reading back over them, I confirmed that when I started this quest for reconciliation, *I hadn't desired it.* I was acting in obedience. I couldn't have been mistaking my own longings for God's, because getting back together with Jeff didn't seem to be what my heart desired. Whenever I decided to go my own way instead of God's, it led me *away from Jeff,* not toward him. I knew Halle was a spiritually mature and wise mentor, and it was difficult to disagree with her, but I had the feeling she was wrong on this one. I did belong with Jeff, almost in spite of myself. Only time would tell.

And then Jeff threw me another bone; he started regularly saying yes to my dinner invitations. It was only about a month after my latest surrender and commitment to obey following the debacle with the softball guy. In fact, the proximity of my surrender and Jeff's turnaround seemed eerily like God telling me, "I told you so." I obeyed, and he came through with a blessing. I wish it were always that simple!

Soon we were together, Jeff and the girls and me, four or five nights every week. He would be at my home or I would be at his, depending on where the girls were staying. We were playing house and family except we did not live in the same home.

I knew Jeff was still uncomfortable with me, because he never asked me to eat dinner at his house. It was always one of the girls who would call and ask. I couldn't help but wonder how much of it was the girls' clever maneuvers and how much truly reflected Jeff's wishes.

Jeff

I'd come a long way since I finally admitted the divorce wasn't all Cheryl's fault and started taking responsibility for my part in our mess of a marriage. So when I allowed myself to begin having dinner at her house, I was cautious yet strangely excited. After we started having dinner together regularly, I battled my feelings constantly. I enjoyed the time we all spent together. I was getting used to being around Cheryl again. I loved the way Brittany and Lauren were so happy when the four of us hung out. It was perfect, actually. But I knew Cheryl wanted more, and I had a hard time going there in my mind. Things were just right, as far as I was concerned.

I became strangely passive because of my ambivalence, allowing Cheryl and the girls to call the shots. Rather than rejecting the efforts by the three of them to get Cheryl and me together, I starting going along with it. I'd let the girls call Cheryl to invite her to dinner, because I couldn't bring myself to do it. I'd pick them up and we'd get in the car, then one of them would say something like, "Let's see if Mommy wants to come." I'd hand over my cell phone and tell them they could ask her to have dinner with us. The truth was, I wanted it too. But I couldn't do it. On my own, I probably wouldn't have been able to make it happen.

One of the issues for me during this period was my sex drive. I'd always been attracted to Cheryl physically, and the last several years hadn't done anything to change that. I never said anything to her about it, but because the time we spent together naturally increased my desire for sex, I constantly battled my desire. Yet (classic male that I am) I knew that if we crossed that line, our relationship would progress from this wishy-washy unidentifiable state to something deeper, and I wasn't sure if I was ready for that. So I kept my struggles to myself.

Three days before Christmas in 1996, I got a call from Cheryl close to midnight. Her voice sounded terrified.

"Cheryl, calm down. What's the matter?"

"I just got back from the Christmas party at the Taylors'," she said, her voice trembling. "My house… Somebody broke in!"

"Are you okay?"

"Well…I called 911. The police are on the way."

"You're sure nobody's in the house?"

"I'm sure."

I'd never heard Cheryl so scared. She was crying and could barely get the words out. I stayed on the phone with her until the police arrived.

"Listen, Cheryl. When the police leave, why don't you call Marci and see if you can stay over there. You shouldn't be alone tonight."

"All right…good idea." She sniffed and tried to calm herself. "Okay, I have to talk to the police now."

We hung up, and I sat there for a minute, torn. I was worried about her, but wasn't sure what I could do to help. I sensed a hope in her that I'd ask her to come to my house, but I didn't know what was appropriate or what I was comfortable with. The phone rang again. It was Claire Taylor, whose Christmas party Cheryl had just come from.

"Hey, Jeff. Have you talked to Cheryl?"

"Yeah…you heard already?"

"She called me first—she didn't know what to do. I told her to call you. What'd you tell her?"

"I told her she should call Marci," I said.

"Jeff, you need to call her back. Ask her to come over to your house."

I was silent.

"Jeff, she needs her family. Let her stay in Brittany's room. Can you do that?"

Claire was right. I needed to let Cheryl be with her girls, if nothing else. It was Christmas, after all.

"All right, Claire. Thanks for the kick in the behind."

"Good night, Jeff."

I called Cheryl back and asked her if she wanted to come over. Her sigh of relief was audible.

"Thank you… I didn't know how I was going to be alone here tonight. I'll be over soon."

Cheryl came over, and because of the holidays, she ended up staying through Christmas and a few more days after that. It was amazing—the feeling of being together as a family over the holidays overwhelmed me. At the same time, I wasn't used to being around her quite that much, so it freaked me out a little bit. There were times I wanted her around and times I didn't. But I was in my own house, so I couldn't leave, and I didn't want to ask her to leave.

I had very mixed emotions. I started to believe that possibly Cheryl had been right, that we should talk about reconciliation. I had to admit we were connecting with each other for the first time in many years. But at the same time, I was thinking, *Are you kidding me? I can't do this.* I grew weary of her constantly saying she felt God leading us toward restoration. I thought she was trying to "play God" by trying to tell me what God wanted. She'd tell me she "felt God leading her" and I'd think, *Oh brother. Once again here's Cheryl trying to control the situation.* Several times I had the ridiculous thought that the break-in had been staged so that Cheryl would have to spend Christmas with me. I brushed that away and then wondered if it had been staged *by God* to bring us together. Then I came to my senses and chalked it up to happenstance; people's houses get broken into all the time.

Ironically, at the same time I felt a pull toward Cheryl. It didn't seem like me, considering the path of pain and anger I'd walked the last few years. So maybe it was from God.

I got the idea that maybe, instead of jumping into anything, we should start dating. Take it one step at a time and go out on dates as if we'd never been married. I tossed that idea around in my mind the whole time she was there and decided that maybe I'd talk to her about it after the new year. But first I wanted to spend a few quiet days, just me and the girls, and make sure this was the right decision.

Cheryl

That was the best Christmas. I didn't know what Jeff thought, but I was incredibly happy to be with my family.

It felt surreal, something I had been praying about for years, our family back under one roof. I was nervous and thought Jeff probably was too. We weren't sure how to act, and it was fairly uncomfortable most of the time. Every morning when I woke up, I wasn't sure where to go. The obvious place was the kitchen for a cup of coffee, but even that seemed awkward. Where was I supposed to sit? I'd brought a couple of cute things to sleep in—nothing too sexy—and I made sure I brushed my hair and teeth before going in the kitchen to greet Jeff.

As the days went by, we grew a tiny bit more comfortable, and Christmas Day was like a dream. We gathered by the tree to open gifts, and I kept gazing at my family and thanking God for the opportunity we had to be together. I made breakfast just like old times. I was filled with hope for the future but scared too. I prayed my bubble would not be burst.

I went home a few days after Christmas. The first half of the girls' winter break was supposed to be *my* time with the girls, but I'd shared it with him. The second half of the break was his, but since we'd had such a fantastic holiday together, I figured he'd call me. I looked forward to spending more time with Jeff and the girls.

Spending the next week completely alone without a single conversation with Jeff was not my idea of a great holiday.

I couldn't believe it after the amazing time we had the week before. The girls called a couple of times, and I left numerous messages on Jeff's answering machine, but to no avail. I tumbled into a state of hopelessness. I had been on such a high and was sure God had orchestrated all of it. I was upset and convinced that Jeff had tricked me. He got to see the girls during "my" week for visitation *and* his. I was furious.

I'm embarrassed to admit that after a week of no contact, I lost my self-control and became obsessed with trying to get hold of Jeff. I wanted to let him know how hurt I was by his deception. I left angry messages, but he never called me back. I finally told him how angry and frustrated I was in a message and begged him to call me. He did, and it was not a pretty picture.

I was mean and insensitive. I would not even let him explain. The conversation ended with us hanging up on each other. For the fiftieth or one-hundredth time (it's so hard to keep track), I made up my mind to move on with my life. I was done with this pursuit. I wanted to get on with things so I could *just live a normal life!*

I was done.

That same day, I went to get my car washed. As I waited for my car, I alternated between stewing and trying to pray. I desperately wanted God to speak to me. I wanted to hear his voice because I couldn't understand what was going on. I had surrendered to him and was following what he'd asked me to do—and now this? It wasn't what I'd bargained for.

After a while, I looked up and a man was standing next to me. He started flirting with me telling me how beautiful I was. By the time my car was ready, he had asked me out on a date, and I'd accepted.

That'll show God, I thought. See? *Other men find me attractive.*

I walked to my car and as I shut my door, there was a knock on my window. It was another guy. I couldn't believe it. I rolled down my window and he handed me his card and told me to call him.

By that point, I was praising God for bolstering my self-esteem. I drove out of the parking lot floating on a cloud, when suddenly my body began to tingle and I recognized what had just happened. I felt almost as though I'd been physically attacked. God was not sending me these distractions to divert me from his instruction. Someone else was involved.

I pulled the car over, closed my eyes, and asked God to forgive me. I was sick of failing tests—and this had been the biggest one ever. With fresh resolve, I humbly accepted my inadequacy and need for God's help, promising to follow him from that day forward no matter what.

I didn't go out with either of the guys from the car wash. And as it turned out, I never dated another guy again.

Jeff

After Cheryl's crazy phone call blasting me for being out of contact, I backed off big time. I'd been so close to considering dating again, but with that kind of behavior, I went back to not wanting to be around her. I fell back into my old pattern of thinking our arrangement was just fine, that I would never consider reconciling with her. I decided once again it was time for us both to move on.

We went back to interacting as we had before. We only saw each other when we exchanged the kids or there was a function we both needed to attend for the girls. For the next three months, my thoughts and emotions pinballed all over the place. I dated someone else, but it was hard to keep my mind off Cheryl. No matter what I did, I couldn't get her out of my head.

Cheryl

One sunny day in spring, I got a phone call. I almost didn't recognize the voice. It was Jeff, and he was stammering. He sounded desperate. He told me he'd been in a collision and asked if I would come. He wasn't hurt, but his car was totaled, and the ambulance was rushing the woman from the other car to the hospital with major injuries. It had been his fault—he never saw her car coming. He was devastated.

The vision from several months ago flashed through my mind. *This is it*, I thought. God told me he would get Jeff's attention. I rushed out the door and headed toward the accident site. I wondered why he had called me and not someone else. But I was going to comfort him. It didn't matter why he called me.

When I got to him, he was sitting in his car, shaking. I hugged him and told him I was there for him no matter what. I told him I loved him. He explained what happened. Thirty minutes passed, and Jeff, with tears in his eyes, looked into my mine and thanked me for coming. I could hardly believe what came out of his mouth next.

"Cheryl, I think God's trying to get my attention." Tears filled my eyes. We knew that God wouldn't cause a car accident and injure an innocent woman simply to "get Jeff's attention." Would he?

I drove Jeff home that morning, pondering the question. Maybe God doesn't cause car accidents, but we know he can take awful circumstances and use them for his good purposes. (See Romans 8:28.) Was that what was happening here?

The woman Jeff had hit was in the hospital for many weeks and nearly died. The whole episode was humbling for Jeff, and he struggled with guilt and remorse. In the long run, it seemed God was using this terrible situation to soften Jeff's heart—toward others, toward me, and toward God himself.

That day started a new phase in our relationship. We spent the day together, and Jeff told me he wanted to begin dating me to see if there might be a chance for us to make our relationship work. He was scared, but that day he became more fearful of God than he was of me! If God was going to use such a tragic occurrence to get Jeff's attention, well, Jeff was going to listen.

I desperately wanted to ask him about Christmas vacation, but before I could, he volunteered the answer. He told me after our time together, he, for the first time in over five years, began to feel as though he was falling in love with me again. He was deathly afraid but decided, because of his commitment to God, that he would approach me right after the holiday to let me know he wanted us to start dating. Because of my overreaction the week after Christmas, he gave up on the whole idea.

I shook my head and realized that if I had stayed out of the way and not tried to *control* the situation, we would have started dating after Christmas.

Instead, I caused a three-month delay. *Note to self: consider your level of commitment to God.*

But now we were going to date, and I felt like I was living in a dream. I was sure we would be on our way to complete reconciliation and a quick remarriage.

In reality, it didn't quite go that way. We started spending considerable time together as a family, and Jeff and I went out on dates once a week or so, but the relationship was slow moving. We got to a place of comfort. Jeff seemed okay with the way it was and in no hurry to progress to the next level.

We struggled with the idea of having sex. We were *acting* like husband and wife except that we didn't live together. We wondered how God viewed our relationship. Were we still married in his eyes? We sought godly counsel and got two diametrically opposing views—that God *did* view us as married and that he didn't. We desired each other desperately, and sometimes we allowed ourselves to make love. And sometimes we held back.

A year passed, and we were still just dating. It had been six years since our divorce was final, and all this time my patience was stretching, growing thinner the longer it was stretched, and building up stronger only to be stretched again.

Jeff

Sometime in 1998, Cheryl sat me down and asked if I thought we were ever going to remarry. She asked what else I needed to know to make a decision. I had known her for eighteen years, after all.

I sat there for a full minute, then looked up. I told her I was scared.

"How can I trust you again, Cheryl? How do I know you won't do the same thing again?"

She seemed shocked. She honestly believed the past was the past and I should be over it.

"I trusted you before," I whispered. "I never thought you'd leave me."

She sat in silence, and I could see her processing. This was something I had noticed was different about her, the way she stopped to think about things rather than simply reacting. Finally she spoke, and her voice was clear and gentle, yet firm. She had a confidence beyond herself.

"Jeff, I'm sorry to say this, but this is not about you. It's not about us anymore." She paused. "It's not about me either. It's about God and his plan for our lives. I never, *never*, want to disappoint my God again."

It was my turn to be shocked. I didn't think Cheryl could come up with an answer that would calm my fears and soothe my soul. But she did. I thought of the words of 2 Corinthians 5:17, that in Christ you're a new creation—the old has gone and the new has come. And that's when the light bulb went on.

She's not the same person she was.

I had been seeing the new Cheryl for years now, and I finally had to face the truth that she was not the same woman I had married in 1982. God was showing me just how new she was—how beautiful, loving, humble, and sexy she was. The recognition was incredibly freeing. I knew God had been at work in both of us and here was the proof that he was truly offering us another chance.

A peace came over me like I'd never known. The godly woman I wanted to believe she had become was *real*. I took her in my arms and I hugged her. I hugged her like I never had before.

ELEVEN

Cheryl
Spring 1998

A few weeks after our emotional conversation, I called Jeff and said there was something I wanted to talk to him about. We met for coffee. I was nervous.

"Jeff, I was thinking…the girls have spring break coming up."

"Right."

"And I was wondering…would you be interested in doing spring break as a family?"

I steeled myself, waiting for the rejection. I'd had this idea in my head for several weeks and had prayed for the guts to stick my neck out and ask him. I knew it was a long shot. We'd been dating and getting along well, but he still needed to take things at his own pace.

Jeff was quiet as I looked at him expectantly, trying not to be too pessimistic.

"Actually, Cheryl, I think that might work."

Did he actually say that? I couldn't believe it.

He continued, "So, did you have any ideas?"

Overwhelmed as I was, I wasn't going to let this opportunity pass. "I was thinking maybe somewhere in Colorado." This was part of my strategy—Colorado was one of Jeff's favorite places. The smile that lit up his face was priceless.

"Like Vail or Breckenridge?" he asked.

"Sure," I said. "I can look into some condos."

We talked about it for a few minutes, excited about the plan. The girls were going to love this!

"Hey, I have an idea," he said. "What if we keep it a surprise for the girls? Maybe not tell them until we're at the airport."

"Oh wow, that's fantastic," I told him. "This is going to be amazing. They'll be so excited!"

We planned our trip to Breckenridge but told the girls it was a vacation for them and Jeff, and that I would drive them to the airport. When I didn't drop them off at the curb, they seemed a little confused. Finally when the four of us were at the gate, Jeff told them I was coming along on the vacation—and the girls went wild. They adored their daddy and always had so much fun with him, but as far as they were concerned, the best times were always with their mom and dad *together*. They almost couldn't believe their good fortune.

Breckenridge, Colorado, is gorgeous any time of year, but that spring it outdid itself. The sky was a brilliant, almost surreal shade of blue, with puffy cotton clouds straight out of a picture book. Snow on the slopes shimmered against the green of the newly emerging grasses and foliage. The quaint little mountain town, a paradise of upscale shops, restaurants, and coffee houses, buzzed with the excitement of people on spring break from all over the country.

Jeff walked down the sidewalk arm-in-arm with Brittany and Lauren, one nine-year-old on either side of him, while I trailed a few steps behind. I smiled watching the three of them, nearly pinching myself at the thought that the four of us were on vacation together. My dream of becoming a family again was *so close* to coming true. We were not married, not living together yet, but spending nearly every day in each other's company.

We spent a week in a condo, and even though things were good between us, the situation still wasn't perfect. Jeff and I slept in separate rooms, not just because we had decided not to have sex, but partly because I sensed the closeness of staying together in one room would have been too much for Jeff. Plus we didn't want to send the wrong message to the girls since we weren't married.

There were moments when he seemed bugged by my presence. And though he was always kind, he still protected himself in small, selfish ways. He took the master bedroom, and I slept in a twin bed in the girls' room. At times, I got overly sensitive, thinking Jeff and the girls were acting like a little team with me on the outside. After all we'd been through, all the anger and pain, it made sense that feeling our way along in this new dynamic might prove difficult. But at the time, it just felt like a big bummer. I wanted to magically get to a place where the four of us functioned as a real family. I kept forgetting we were in the midst of trying to create a new normal. We were blazing new territory, trying to be a family, and yet...not. The hardest part was not knowing whether we'd *ever* be a real family again, or if this was it.

Jeff and I had some romantic moments, and I could tell he felt the intimacy too. We were talking and connecting on so many levels we hadn't experienced before. For me it was wonderful, but Jeff was still scared by our new closeness. He needed time to get used to it.

When the vacation was over, for all its rough patches, Jeff and I seemed to have an understanding—a bond—that was more profound than anything we'd had before. His smile, so warm and tender, and his gentle kiss as he said good-bye at my house told me that maybe I could finally stop worrying. It was slow going, but we were headed in the right direction.

Jeff
Late 1998–Early 1999

Months passed while Cheryl and I continued "dating," but it didn't look like any dating relationship I'd ever seen. We'd known each other for two decades, shared sheets for nearly ten years, seen each other at our very worst, held hands through the birth of our daughters, yet I walked her to the doorstep as if we were teenagers. It was strange terrain, and we had no role models to help us navigate it. We took it day by day.

One sunny winter afternoon as I drove home from the airport after a business trip, I was struck by how much I was looking forward to seeing my girls—all three of them. What an amazing yet scary feeling. My mind wandered over the last several months since the trip to Breckenridge. Certain ordinary moments stood out as tiny milestones, bright markers on this road to who-knew-where.

There was the Sunday I sat in church, listening to the sermon. I glanced to my left to see Brittany and Lauren—miraculously paying attention—and Cheryl sitting on the other side of them. It struck me as bizarre. *We are in church together.* It felt right. It felt normal. It was such a small thing, but the impact on me was profound.

A few weeks went by, and it was early fall. We stood in the Texas Rangers ballpark, the smell of foot-long hot dogs permeating the air and the screams of wild fans all around. The 1998 baseball season had been exciting in Dallas, with the Rangers headed for the American League West championships. The atmosphere pulsated with enthusiasm as our team took the lead. I was flanked by Cheryl, my daughters, and Cheryl's parents, and we all had our arms around each other singing a rousing rendition of "Take Me Out to the Ball Game" at the seventh-inning stretch. I wondered, *Is it just a sports-induced high?* But no. It was an awesome moment. *This* was what I wanted my life to look like.

A few weeks later we were at the lake house I'd bought several years before. Raking the colorful autumn leaves was something the girls and I always did together. This cottage was my getaway, a haven I'd only shared with the girls. Brittany and Lauren played in the leaf piles, ruining them almost as fast as I could build them. I looked up from my rake, shaking my head, and shared a knowing grin with Cheryl. How strange. Cheryl was the last person I thought I'd ever invite to the lake house. But she fit right in.

Another month passed, and it was early Christmas morning. The girls were still asleep in their room at my house as I dialed the phone.

"Hello?" Cheryl's sleepy voice answered.

"Merry Christmas," I told her.

"Jeff!" Her voice was instantly alert. "Merry Christmas! Are the girls up yet?"

"Nope, but it won't be long."

"They're pretty excited to see what Santa brought." Her voice held a wistful note.

"It's not the same for them without you," I admitted. "You want to come over?"

Cheryl was silent for a long second. "Are you sure, Jeff? This is your day."

I didn't want to make a big deal of it. "Yeah, I'm sure. Get over here."

She must have broken land-speed records because she was there just a few minutes later, before the girls had opened any of the gifts. It was our family's best Christmas yet.

Sometime after the beginning of the new year, I sat talking to Bill, a good friend who'd supported me throughout the last several years. I told him how things were getting much better between me and Cheryl. He looked at me in that challenging way he had.

"Have you forgiven her?"

"You would have to ask that." I shook my head.

"The hard questions are usually the most important."

"I know, I know." I thought for a moment. "Yes, I've forgiven her…and I've been trying to leave it behind me. But then in odd moments it all comes up, and I'm as mad as ever."

"Maybe that's why Jesus said we had to forgive—"

"Seventy times seven. I know. So I just have to keep doing it over and over."

"Well, yeah. And keep praying about it. I don't think it's the kind of thing you can do on your own."

"That's for sure. I couldn't have forgiven her in my own strength. It's been all God." I shook my head. "I'm way too stubborn."

"Most of us are, buddy. We have too much ego. That's why we need help with this stuff."

"Bottom line: it's a choice. If I keep choosing forgiveness, at some point maybe I'll be done with it."

Not long after that, I woke one morning feeling like a weight had lifted from my chest. It was the weight of bitterness…and it was gone. Forgiveness had been a long road, and I couldn't be sure I'd never have another rough moment, but this was the first time I felt I'd actually achieved it.

Now, driving home from the airport, I wondered what had finally made the forgiveness "stick." I thought it must have been my choice to keep trusting God in this crazy situation. I'd also realized this journey was much more a spiritual one than anything else. Beyond the emotional and psychological part, beyond the part about Cheryl and me, the journey was about my decision to pursue God and trust him. Ironically, Cheryl had been telling me the same thing about her own journey for years.

I pulled up to Cheryl's house and felt a surge of happiness as I walked to the porch. For the first time since I could remember, the joy wasn't marred by anger or resentment. It was pure. The grudge against Cheryl appeared to have evaporated.

Cheryl
April 1999

Spring arrived, and with it came a powerful feeling of renewal. For the past few months, Jeff and I had been clicking incredibly well, and I couldn't have been happier. We were still just dating and hadn't made any moves in the marriage direction, but I was getting better at this patience thing. We seemed to be headed in the right direction, and I was content. Besides, I'd decided to be content *whether or not* things were going my way. It was all part of my growing faith. So my demeanor around Jeff was much more relaxed these days.

What continually surprised and delighted me was how much I truly loved hanging out with him. I wanted to be with him more than I wanted to be with anyone else.

It was spring break again, and the girls were at a friend's house for the night. Jeff and I had a great evening, with dinner and a movie, just enjoying each other's company. We sat on the sofa, talking and laughing about the movie we'd seen. Then Jeff changed the subject.

"So…I notice you haven't mentioned getting married in a while."

I grinned and tried to make light of it. "Well, why ruin a good thing?"

His brow furrowed. "Do you still think it's the direction we should be headed?"

I looked in his eyes and nodded. "I do, Jeff. With all my heart." He looked at me, and we both burst out laughing.

I do. What a choice of words.

He took a deep breath. "I think...I might be getting there, Cheryl. Can you be patient with me a little longer?"

I wrapped my arms around him and held him tight. "Just try not to make it another six and a half years, okay?"

June 1999

Two months later, while the girls were away at summer camp, Jeff and I sat in a restaurant. We were having a good time, but Jeff seemed slightly...off. I couldn't tell if he was nervous, preoccupied with a work issue, or what. I hoped I hadn't done something to upset him.

"Is everything okay, Jeff?"

He gave me a startled look. "Sure. How's your pasta?"

I shook my head. That was weird. "Pasta's delicious." I squinted at him. Something was up; I knew it.

"Jeff—"

He held up his hand.

"Cheryl." He paused. "Do you think we could have a better marriage the second time around?"

Talk about a question almost blowing you out of your chair.

"Absolutely. Yes, I know we could. We're both different people now, don't you think?"

He nodded. "Are you sure you don't want this just for the girls?" he asked.

I reached across the table and put my hand over his. "I'd be lying if I said the girls had nothing to do with it. Of course the idea of having our family together and raising the girls together is the most amazing thing ever. I want that so much. But it's you, Jeff. It's you I want to be with. I couldn't do it just for the kids. They'll be moving out in eight more years, and it's you I'd still be living with. That's what I want. I want a life with you."

He held my hand, and I thought I saw his eyes glistening.

"Then, Cheryl…will you marry me?"

What can one say about a seven-year dream coming true?

When Jeff and I looked at each other across that table and he smiled at me, I thought my heart would erupt right out of my chest. Neither of us could stop grinning, and we were nearly overcome with emotion. The evening continued as we discussed plans and dreams and how to tell the kids.

Just thinking of how happy Brittany and Lauren would be filled my heart with the most incredible joy. Jeff felt the same way. We talked about not only rebuilding our marriage, but also recreating our family. I don't have words for what an extraordinary feeling it was.

We had often heard people talking about keeping a marriage together "for the children." We didn't believe it was possible if the children were the *only* motivator, but we'd learned that children could be a powerful motivation to keep a marriage together or bring it back from the edge. How amazing was God's design of the family! People all over the world, of every religion or no religion at all, know deep within that the family unit is powerful and the presence of children can be the glue that holds husbands and wives together when all else fails.

So we spent the rest of the evening plotting how we were going to give Brittany and Lauren the best news of their lives so far.

A couple of days later, we picked up our ten-year-olds from summer camp. They tumbled into the car with all their gear and dirt and bruises and stories of their week. It was an hour-and-a-half drive home, so I waited until the girls settled down. Then I got their attention.

"Girls, I think Daddy has something to say."

"What? What, Daddy? What is it?"

Jeff turned his head and grinned. "Nah, I think I changed my mind."

They saw the wide smile on my face and knew something was up.

"Da-a-a-a-a-dd-y-y-y-y!"

"Okay, I'll tell you what," Jeff offered. "You girls be calm for the rest of the drive, and then Mom and I have a secret to tell you at home. Deal?"

"No way, Daddy! Tell us now!" Lauren cried.

Brittany was a little more suspicious. "What's it about? Is it something good?" she wanted to know.

I turned to the girls. "I promise: this is one of the best things you've ever heard."

They squealed. "Are we going to Hawaii? Did we get a puppy?"

They spent the remainder of the drive trying to guess what our secret was, but Jeff and I refused to give any clues. Since we had been spending so much time together, it would have made sense if the girls guessed we were getting remarried. But in fact—although they dreamed and schemed for our family to be reunited—they were so accustomed to our "family-but-not-a-family" they'd all but stopped believing it could truly happen. In truth, this was the biggest heartbreak of my life, and I looked forward to helping them heal and put all of the trauma behind them. All of this combined with my anticipation of sharing this news with them made for one of the most nerve-wracking few hours I'd ever experienced.

Once we got home, we were barely in the door before they were all over us.

"Tell us! Tell us!"

Jeff and I stood close together and waited a moment to keep them in suspense. I looked at Jeff and nodded.

"Okay, girls, here it is," he said in a solemn tone. Their expectant faces looking up at us were priceless. "Mom and I…have decided…"

"What? What?"

He looked back at me. "We…"

"…are getting remarried…"

"…to each other."

There was a split second of silence while it sunk in. Disbelief filled their faces—then chaos broke loose. Brittany gasped, just stood there holding onto the edge of the counter, speechless. Her mouth dropped open and her eyes went wide as she looked back and forth between us. My eyes had already filled with tears and she seemed to realize that she'd really heard what she thought.

"Are you serious?" Her voice cracked as huge tears began to stream down her face. Then she simply buckled in the knees and Jeff and I literally had to hold her up.

Lauren stood paralyzed watching us as if afraid it was a joke. She'd been praying about it for so long—the majority of her childhood, in fact—her brain simply wouldn't let her believe it was finally coming true.

Her eyes filled. "Really?" she whispered, searching our faces as tears spilled over onto her cheeks. Then she exploded, running around Jeff's house, laughing and whooping in excited disbelief, and calling out, "Do you mean it? Do you really? Is it for real?" She whipped around from a corner, and leaped at Jeff, flying into his arms.

As Brittany sobbed and hugged me I marveled again at how different their personalities were. Jeff and I circled our arms around each other and them. And we stood there with tears streaming down our faces. The world went by outside the door, but all we needed was right here. Everything else faded in a moment of blissful perfection, and I thought I understood what heaven must be like.

Thank you, God. Thank you.

We planned the wedding for the girls' fall break in October, four months later. The time leading up to it was heady with the excitement of making plans and preparing to move me into Jeff's house. It was an unbelievably happy time, and Jeff and I spent much of it marveling at how God had worked in our lives. Looking back over our journey, it was difficult to believe all that had happened.

We had so much fun "going public" with our news. Most of our friends probably expected it—we were together so often, and people saw us all over town. Many had been praying faithfully for us for years, and it must have been gratifying to witness the answer to their fervent prayers. It was so heartwarming to see almost everyone visibly excited for us. Our close friends had been with us through all the rough times, and they told us how beautiful our story was and how they knew it had to be God's doing. Some of our friends had seen no hope of us ever reconciling, so they felt they saw a miracle happen right in front of their eyes. A few friends even apologized to me for the times they'd tried to dissuade me from my dogged pursuit of restoration. They had tried to get me to move on, telling me that Jeff would never come around. Those friends became our strongest supporters because they'd seen God working first-hand.

There were a few people who were not happy at all. A small group of

Jeff's friends didn't understand how Jeff could forgive me and take me back. They'd seen Jeff devastated and broken and did not believe it was appropriate to excuse behavior like mine. They didn't understand the intense spiritual journey we'd both been on, and they couldn't see the miracles of Jeff's softened heart and my profound commitment to God and Jeff. All they saw was Jeff unwisely setting himself up for a repeat disaster.

I understood their perspective, even though it was painful. None of us is capable of forgiving such scandalous actions without God working in us. And as Jeff and I found out, it's a long road even when we pray about it every single day. Those friends soon moved away, and we lost touch with them. I've since learned that this is a common scenario when a marriage is on the rocks and friends are forced to take sides. Once they choose, they sometimes find it hard to accept both halves of "the couple" again. This is an unfortunate reality we simply have to accept.

The fact that we were getting remarried was humbling, even for our friends. It just seemed like an impossible thing. Right away we began telling people, "We didn't do this. God did."

That October, we headed to the small resort of Beaver Creek, high in the Rocky Mountains. We didn't take anyone with us except Brittany and Lauren. This was about our family—husband and wife, parents and children.

There is nothing quite so magnificent as a crisp, cold, autumn day in Colorado. The radiance of the blue sky was stunning, and the bright sun felt like God himself smiling down on us, celebrating the culmination of his own incredible work in the last seven years.

We walked into the chapel, all four of us holding hands. I glanced at the girls' faces and saw their individual personalities perfectly expressed—

Brittany so serious, tears already threatening to spill over, and Lauren solemn but letting out a smile every now and then, a combination of disbelief and joy apparent on her face. My eyes lifted to Jeff's, and I saw my future there. My life, my love.

As we spoke our vows to one another, I was profoundly humbled. The enormity of God's grace was overwhelming, and my gratefulness was overpowering. I felt like I was living a dream; the sun was brighter than I'd ever seen it, the air itself sparkling. It was cold outside, yet we could feel a warmth through our bodies...almost as if we could feel God inside each of us.

When the brief ceremony was over, the intensity of the moment overtook us all, and we sobbed, not holding back, finally free to express the fullness of our hearts. How can I explain what it's like to truly experience a miracle? None of us had any words.

Brittany and Lauren clung to us but were careful not to get *between* us. In fact, they made sure Jeff and I were physically connected at all times—holding hands or standing with our bodies pressed together. With the deep, pure wisdom of children, they understood the magnitude of what God had done, and they knew we would need to be vigilant in rebuilding and protecting our "new" family.

That was truly the first day of the rest of our lives. As Brittany, Lauren, Jeff, and I stood locked in an indescribably joyful embrace, none of us wanted to let go.

And in fact, we never have.

TWELVE

Cheryl
1999 and Beyond

Our wedding wasn't the end of the story, obviously. It was just the beginning. Over the next few years we learned much more about building a healthy marriage. We had already seen how God takes the trauma in our lives and uses it "for the good of those who love him" (Romans 8:28). We'd learned about trusting God even when it seemed crazy to do so, and we'd seen firsthand the amazing power of forgiveness. Together Jeff and I had discovered the deep, soul-satisfying pleasure of a strong, intact family. Moving forward, we were about to encounter whole new levels of intimacy and honesty as we sought to create a solid marriage from the ground up, with Jesus as our foundation.

As we began our new life together, we figured out there were two distinct phases to restoring a broken relationship. First we had to heal from the trauma of the breakup itself—the affair and all the pain we inflicted on each other in the divorce. Even people who don't get divorced have to work on repairing the damage done during the angry times. This is the pain closest to the surface, so it usually needs to be dealt with before getting to deeper issues.

The second part of the restoration is looking back and dealing honestly with all the reasons the relationship started going downhill in the first place. It's easy to stall on this second part. Once we feel like we've gotten past the immediate trauma, it's tempting to leave it at that. It takes diligence to look back and uncover the original issues that led to unhappiness, drifting apart, unfaithfulness, anger, or loss of love.

To be honest, even after all we'd come through together, Jeff and I found this necessary work a drag sometimes. It required looking back at a time when we desperately wanted to simply *look forward*. It was hard to face the past, admit the things we'd done wrong, and talk about strategies for avoiding those mistakes. We'd both come so far in our spiritual journey that it was tempting to simply quote scripture—"The old has gone, the new has come!"—and focus on the future (see 2 Corinthians 5:17). But our intense desire to *never* repeat the past gave us the motivation to work through those issues even when it was unpleasant.

Throughout our seven years apart, Jeff and I had followed individual paths in our walk with God, during which we'd mostly healed from the pain of the affair and the divorce. We'd also spent considerable time thinking hard about *what went wrong* in our first marriage, so that we could learn how to avoid repeating it. We'd gone through thought processes of blaming the other, then accepting responsibility ourselves. Once we were remarried, it was time to bring together all the things we'd learned to create a new model for our marriage.

Jeff

The hardest thing for me was to understand exactly how deep Cheryl's loneliness and despair had been in our first marriage. I knew it had to be profound, and what scared me was wondering whether I could live up to her expectations and fulfill her needs the second time around if I'd so completely missed really knowing her the first time. I had to look closely at myself to recognize just what I'd contributed to the suffering she'd endured.

I realized I had completely abdicated any responsibility to see my wife for who she was and to care about her heart. How could I avoid these fatal mistakes in the future?

The only answer was spending time intentionally getting to know Cheryl on a whole new level. I had to discover that emotional connection she was missing all those years. I learned to slow down my life enough to sit and talk to my wife, to listen to her heart, care about her—and not always try to fix it! Just as importantly, she wanted to know what was going on inside me, what my thoughts and feelings were. I had to learn a new language of talking about my hopes, dreams, expectations, and fears. But I did finally get it.

Connecting at a deeper level is a much more satisfying way to have a relationship, but it definitely doesn't come naturally to a lot of men. Guys are supposed to be strong—getting too emotional or going to counseling is a sign of weakness in our culture. And many people don't perceive men as having the need to connect at a deeper level. I think we do have that need, and a lot of times we don't realize it. Men sure don't talk about it. It turns out the willingness to open up and connect on deep levels with your wife is one of the best things a guy can do to keep his marriage healthy. Who knew?

So Cheryl and I had to learn to pull out all the stops and talk to each other—gut level. It wasn't just hard for me; it was hard for Cheryl too. She'd learned early in our first marriage that trying to talk to me about the issues of her heart got her nowhere, so she was overcoming a couple decades of conditioning.

We had to be intentional about all this "talking" we were supposed to do. We'd go out to dinner, and instead of talking about the kids or what was happening down at church, we'd make the effort to "check in" with each other. We learned that often the answer to "how are you?" was "fine" at first, but if we probed, we could get a truer answer out of each other. One of the biggest things to learn—and we're still improving on this one—was how to speak up immediately if something hurt us or bothered us. Letting things fester was a huge enemy to the relationship!

Cheryl

One of the most common questions people asked us after we remarried was, "Why does your marriage work now when it didn't work then?" The biggest answer is that Jeff and I learned to take the focus off ourselves. Our lives are not about our own immediate desires. Our lives are about what God wants for us, what's best for our family and our marriage. We try to live by the saying, "It's not about me."

But in a funny sort of paradox, we've also learned the opposite—when there seems to be an issue in the relationship, it usually helps to take the focus off the marriage and for each of us to look at ourselves. *How is my heart? What's going on in my mind? How is my relationship with the Lord? Am I living with purpose, with integrity, with passion?* In many cases, you can start to get answers to the problem right there. Sometimes we have to say, "It's not about the marriage; it's not about my spouse; it's about me." In order for the relationship to work, I have to get my stuff together as an individual.

But it's never just about me alone or Jeff alone. It's about me and God. It's about Jeff and God. How well are we staying in touch with him? How well are we following him? It's about our relationships with the Lord. In an interesting way, this seems to take the pressure off of us. I know Jeff's most important relationship is with God, not with me. He knows the same about me. So it takes the pressure off our marriage because we know we don't have to fill all of each other's needs.

Another reason our marriage works now is because, having been through all those years of turmoil, we no longer take each other for granted, and we don't take the marriage for granted. We realize that each day we have to create it all over again. We also communicate better than we did in the past. We don't let minor disagreements blow up; we address them when they happen and don't let them fester. We don't let dissatisfaction build. We try to recognize it when it first starts and get to the root of the problem.

My friend Laura has walked a path of reconciliation and restoration and says the issue that gave her the most trouble was that of "feelings." They come and go, don't they? Sometimes it's hard to stay motivated to keep your marriage strong when you can't seem to muster up those lovin' feelings.

Obviously, love is a choice. But even when you know that, depending on where you are, making the choice can feel impossible. It comes back to the same thing. *This isn't about me; it's about obedience to the Lord.* While I walked through my seven years of being divorced, I found that as I continued in obedience, the feelings came. When I first started to pursue reconciliation in obedience to God's desires, I sure didn't *feel* love for Jeff! But I did love God. And that was enough to keep me going in the right direction. One way to think about it is do what you *know*, and the feelings will follow.

How do we discipline ourselves to walk in obedience and not waiver? How do we rise above the pain enough to attain the rewards of an obedient life? We *decide*. We *choose* to take the higher road no matter how great the pain. We *decide* to white-knuckle it at times. We *decide*, after we've failed, to pull ourselves back up—to allow God to pull us back up—and continue doing what's right. It takes self-discipline and commitment. It takes desire. And that desire needs to be about loving God enough to do it his way. We don't have to desire to do the right thing. We just have to desire God enough.

When we're dealing with feelings in marriage, we sometimes need to change our perspective and ask ourselves, "What are my feelings trying to tell me?" When Jeff and I were married the first time, I felt discontented and lonely. But I never took the time—or the risk—to honestly face what my feelings clearly told me about my needs and the shallowness of my marriage. God can use our feelings to take us to a new place. There have been times when I've had to pray and ask God, *What are you trying to tell me through these feelings?*

The bottom line is that our feelings are important indicators of where our hearts are, what we're missing, what we need. But feelings don't always lead us in the right direction if we take them at face value. We need to take our feelings seriously and examine them, without always following where they lead. Regardless of our feelings, the key is to make choices, each and every day, to be obedient.

Jeff

Cheryl and I experienced a situation common among couples having trouble. Usually one spouse wants to save the marriage while the other's heart isn't in it. It takes two to save a marriage. But even if both spouses aren't ready and willing, the marriage may not be hopeless.

It's ironic that I would say this. During the last eighteen months of our first marriage, I was desperately trying to salvage it, but Cheryl wouldn't budge. Back then I would have told you, "If your spouse isn't coming to the party, forget it. You're finished." I absolutely couldn't save my marriage by myself, no matter how much I begged, pleaded, stonewalled, or bought gifts. Even a dream house on a golf course couldn't do the trick.

So why do I believe it's not hopeless? Because when the tables turned in our situation and it was Cheryl who wanted to salvage the marriage when I was uninterested, it was *Cheryl's perseverance plus God's intervention* that brought us back together. I wanted no part in reconciliation for a good five years after the divorce. But it still happened. How could that be?

Patience, perseverance, endurance, and prayer. Those were the things Cheryl needed. She had to stand on faith and wait—and keep waiting even when she wanted to give up over and over again. She had to keep asking God for direction, and when she felt God confirming restoration, she had to keep fighting for it.

But here's the thing. We wouldn't have gotten back together if I hadn't experienced a change of heart. As important as persistence is for the one who wants to save the marriage, a change of heart is equally crucial for the unwilling one. If there's no honest change of heart, no sincere willingness to try to make it work, then a reconciliation isn't going to work.

As we've already mentioned, this "change of heart" doesn't mean the feelings necessarily line up with reconciliation. It doesn't mean both spouses are *in love* and want to make it work. It means both spouses have turned their hearts and minds toward God and the desire to follow him and are willing to let him lead the way.

If you're the one persevering and hoping for a change of heart in your unresponsive spouse, how much time do you give it? That's one of the most difficult questions. From our experience, I can only say I believe you have to keep persisting as long as you sense confirmation from God that you are to pursue restoration. God allowed Cheryl and me to suffer in divorce for seven years, and I know he did that for a reason. It's not unusual for a couple to "work on their marriage" for two months and then give up. When they meet Cheryl and me and they realize it took us seven years, they find a new perspective. God's timing is different from ours!

Cheryl's persistence was an enormous factor in my eventual ability to forgive her. The way she hung in there and kept pursuing reconciliation was truly mind boggling at times, and I knew there had to be more than simply her own determination at work. I figured she must truly be following God's leading in her life. Her persistence, along with seeing what a sincere, faith-filled person she'd become, reeled me in. Eventually, everything she did and said confirmed that not only did she love God deeply and wholly, she loved *me*.

Cheryl

Once Jeff and I were remarried, I looked back over our seven years apart and saw that God dealt with me in phases, layering the lessons on top of each other as I began to understand them. For a time the lesson was perseverance and discovering how to keep running the race even when I was exhausted to my bones. Then it was the process of surrender. I surrendered over and over, and each time it got deeper, more genuine. I relinquished my right to do things *my way*. I had to learn to trust that God knew better than I did.

Then it got to the issue of obedience. That was the biggest lesson of the seven years. That's what this was all about. Was I willing to stand with God, doing the right thing, trusting that the blessings would come in due time?

None of this would have been possible without the message that was under it all—how much God loves us, how much he's given us, how much he's forgiven us. That I could be guilty of such terrible sins and yet feel his love unmistakably—that had a bigger impression on me than anything in my life.

I got to the point where, even if Jeff and I never got back together, I was committed not to remarry. I trusted God that he was leading me to reconcile with Jeff, and I wouldn't have done anything to obstruct his plan. Even if Jeff had remarried, I knew I'd have to stay single. Who knows if, forty years later, we would have reconciled on our deathbeds? My trust in God had to be so total that I was fine with that. This is what taught me the meaning of surrender. I truly, wholeheartedly desired God's will instead of my own.

It's hard to say all this without sounding self-righteous. I'm far from perfect! My determination is not always strong, my understanding of God is woefully incomplete. I still have moments when I question God's will for me or I seek him and can't seem to hear his voice. I'm just like any normal person. I feel privileged that God allowed me a unique experience of marriage reconciliation so that others can possibly find renewed hope for their own marriages.

Jeff

It was Cheryl's idea for us to go into marriage ministry. She felt God calling us into it and came to me with the idea.

But I wasn't ready. Sound familiar? Seems like for most of this story Cheryl was out ahead with grand ideas and I was somewhere behind, dragging my feet. But I couldn't do it. Once again, the timing wasn't right for me. For everything there is a season—and that wasn't the season for me to be ministering to others about marriage.

I continued working with the youth at church, and not only did I love it, I knew I was good at it. I saw results with these kids. I watched them grow spiritually and every other way, and it was incredibly gratifying. As Cheryl gently encouraged me to move in a new direction, I realized I was prideful about my work with the youth and wanted to hold on to that. I began praying about it and felt God trying to show me that possibly the youth leadership was becoming an idol. I was too wrapped up in my own success there and didn't want to let it go.

But soon God impressed on me that he'd done a miraculous work in putting our marriage back together and he wanted me to give him the glory. The way to give him the glory is by telling other people what he did in our lives. So I needed to switch my focus from the youth work to exploring marriage ministry. A little more than two years after our wedding, we began building Hope Matters Marriage Ministries.

Cheryl

One of the most valuable resources in our ministry is a book by Gary Thomas titled *Sacred Marriage*. I can't tell you how often we wished this book had been around when we were struggling so much! But I trust God knew what he was doing. Both Jeff and I are so stubborn, chances are we would have had a hard time accepting the book's message. Put simply, it's this: "What if God designed marriage not to make us happy, but to make us holy?"

When I first read this question, it made me angry. I was already remarried to Jeff and had supposedly "matured" spiritually through all those years of seeking God, but this message still didn't sit well with me. All my life I thought one of the purposes of marriage was to make me happy. Even after I'd learned so much about God's view of relationships and his purposes for marriage, I still wanted to believe that God *wanted* me to be happy.

But after reading the book and reflecting on the journey we'd gone through, I realized this could be the most profound teaching on marriage I'd ever heard, except for the Bible itself. The book underscores what Jeff and I had discovered: if we're focusing on ourselves—our own wants, needs, opinions—we may be missing the greatest blessing of marriage.

It was ironic that I had to learn to love God and seek him before I could repair my marriage, because Gary Thomas's book is about how marriage itself is designed to help us know God better, trust him and love him. We had to realize from experience what *Sacred Marriage* was saying, that marriage isn't as much about me and my spouse as it is about me and God.

For the last several years, we've conducted Sacred Marriage classes in our home, using Thomas's book. We watch couples come in to the first meeting, and if their marriage isn't going well, we can see it in their body language. They don't touch; they barely look at each other. When we introduce the concept of Sacred Marriage, the immediate responses are frequently negative. They'll tell us, "I hate this title. I'm not reading this book." Jeff and I recognize their anger and stubbornness! Our approach is to be gentle with them and let them know they're loved. We want them to know that we understand where they're coming from. We gently encourage them to give the book a try and be committed to coming to class.

It's so amazing how God works, because invariably we see paradigm shifts happening with the couples in our classes. They start to realize, "It really isn't all about me." By the end of the fourteen-week class, these couples have shifted. They have a unity that wasn't evident in the beginning. You can tell they're moving forward together. They have something new on which to base their marriage. The combination of hearing Jeff's and my story and learning the concepts of Sacred Marriage really seems to give people renewed hope.

And that is the most amazing thing of all! Throughout my seven-year trek through the wilderness, I kept hearing God say that this was all for his glory. And I always wondered, what the heck does that mean? Sounds nice and religious, but really… how does it apply to my life? Now he is getting all the credit for taking our marriage, something that was beyond dead, and resurrecting it. That's what he meant by "for his glory"! He's also chosen to work through Jeff and me to revive, repair, and restore countless other marriages. What an honor!

~

If you had asked me eighteen years ago, as I was pursuing divorce, if I thought my marriage could be reconciled no matter what stage it was in, my answer would have been a resounding NO! Most couples believe there is a point when the situation becomes hopeless. But I am here to tell you it's not true. Jesus promised that seeking reconciliation will bear fruit, so there is great hope that a marriage can be restored to a place beyond what a couple could even imagine.

Webster's dictionary defines *reconciliation* as "the process of making consistent or compatible." To reconcile is "to cause to cease hostility or opposition; to harmonize or settle; to restore; to cause a person to accept or be resigned to something not desired." This word meant nothing to me until God began showing me how it applied to my marriage.

Could this mean that a marriage that's in shambles or that no longer exists can be made brand-new? That is absolutely what it is saying! Knowing and believing that God gave us the ministry of reconciliation, we can conclude that his plan for a reconciled marriage is to make a couple compatible, to cease hostility or opposition between them, to harmonize or settle them, to restore their relationship, and to cause them to accept or be resigned to something they may not desire. I never dreamed that, once Jeff and I were divorced, our marriage could be restored to something "infinitely more than we would ever dare to ask or hope" (Ephesians 3:20, NLT). But God did it. He is bigger than all our problems. He is a God of hope. And after all…hope matters.

A Conversation with Brittany and Lauren

Our daughters, Brittany and Lauren, are our greatest blessings and the loves of our lives. They not only lived this entire story with us but played significant parts and were a vital factor in our reconciliation. God used our love for our girls to keep us in contact with each other nearly every day throughout our divorced years. That love was one thing we always had in common, so that no matter what other emotions were coursing through us, we were parents together.

For that reason, we wanted to give Brittany and Lauren their own voices here. We wanted them to have the opportunity to speak freely about how our journey affected their lives. They were four years old when we divorced and eleven when we remarried.

We've made it a habit to be honest with the girls about what happened between us in an age-appropriate way. They were thirteen when they learned the most devastating part of the story—that I (Cheryl) had an affair. I'd been praying that God would give me the right time to tell them, and then Brittany asked me flat out, "Did you have an affair?" I explained it to them, in eighth-grader terms, while I sobbed. It was very difficult, coming clean before my precious daughters. And it was hard for them to know the truth about their mom. But it was freeing to finally have the whole story out on the table, and I believe my willingness to be honest has had profound effects on my relationships with them.

Today they're twenty years old and absolutely the light of our lives. Our editors asked them a few questions, and they were happy to give their perspective on this story that defined their childhood.

How did it feel when you learned your parents were getting back together?

Brittany: When my parents told us they were getting back together, I almost fainted. I had literally prayed every night for this. I cannot even describe the happiness and joy I felt when I found out.

Lauren: I'm not really sure how I felt at the moment; it was a mix of many emotions. This restoration was full of the power of God. It was almost surreal. I knew I had seen Jesus work a miracle.

What do you remember about life after the divorce?

Brittany: I remember my dad coming to pick me up during the week at my mom's house. We went home after school with my mom and then switched off houses evenly during the week. I was always excited to see Daddy. He usually cooked pasta or ravioli, and we had Italian names to go along with the meal. We always had fun at my dad's house, but I wanted to be with my mom whenever we were away from her, and the same situation happened when were away from my dad. I remember feeling sad when I had to leave the other parent because I realized they would be alone.

Lauren: I constantly wanted unity for our family. I frequently felt worried because I could tell my parents were hurting, and I hated that. I remember wanting to be like the other kids at school whose parents were married. I didn't want to be confused about what address to write when I was filling out papers; I wanted to know I was going to one house when I left at the end of the day.

Brittany: When I look back on the years of the divorce, I realize that my parents were always looking out for Lauren and me. They were never selfish.

They cared deeply about spending time with us and would drop any of their plans for us. I loved the lake house with my dad, but I always wished that my mom could come and have the memories with us. I was also so thankful for my mom because she was extremely dedicated to my sister and me. She picked us up every day from school and was always there for us and with us. I know she struggled financially, but she didn't give up time with us.

Lauren: It was my dream for my parents to reconcile. It seemed like an impossible miracle to me, but I had hope because I watched my mom hope, and I watched my dad submit to the Lord to soften his heart. I prayed for them to get back together every single night. My friends and I always talked about how much we all wanted it.

Brittany: I think getting our parents back together was probably one of the biggest things I thought about while I was young.

Were you ever angry at your parents about the divorce?

Brittany: I was angry at some point during the divorce, but I didn't express my anger in clear ways. I think it came up in other behaviors, like reacting impulsively to trivial situations, being short with my parents, or sometimes being rude to kids at school when I was younger. Deep down, I still understood that divorce was not the plan for the family that God intended.

Lauren: I definitely did as a child; I would get very impatient and frustrated that they would not consider getting back together when I would ask. I would get angry at their pride and stubbornness because in my mind I didn't understand why they wouldn't want peace in the family like I did. In that sense, I felt like I took on the parent role. I don't have anger about the divorce today because we were very nurtured by our parents, even though they were apart. We were definitely their first priority, which in my opinion, especially from observing other divorce situations, is a key component in reducing resentment. My parents also encouraged us to talk about our feelings and cared so much about us that my emotions never got to the point where they turned into anger.

Brittany: We didn't know about the affair until after they were remarried to each other. If I'd known while they were still apart, I probably would have been angrier with my mom. But when I learned the whole truth, I already understood that her life without Christ had been completely different and that Jesus had redeemed and restored her. I don't have any anger now because I've seen the restoration and power of Christ in all of our lives as a family.

Lauren: God brought our whole family through this trial to draw us closer to each other and to the Lord. In seeing the purpose of this divorce, I can't help but be thankful because of the many lives that are transformed through the ministry and hearing my parents' story.

How did the divorce affect your general feeling of safety and security as a child?

Lauren: Both of my parents were constantly trying to make it as "easy" as possible for us. A dad's role in a girl's life is essential to feeling secure, and my dad showed me my self-worth and taught me to find it in the Lord. My mom was always there to nurture and comfort, which also aided in my feeling of safety.

Brittany: Honestly, it's hard for me to recall, but I know I didn't feel stability going from house to house. I probably questioned where I was going to be at any given time. Yet the selflessness of both my parents provided comfort when I felt unstable.

Lauren: At times I remember feeling unstable in the fact that our family was not the way God intended for it to be. Even as a child, I could feel the weight of the consequences of divorce. I experienced a lot of fear as a child.

What was it like going back and forth between your parents' homes?

Lauren: It was miserable! It was such a hassle in the insignificant things. I remember forgetting parts of outfits or homework for the next day of school, and we would have to find a way to get everything. Every time we switched houses, I had strong feelings of dysfunction. I just wanted to stay in one house with everyone together and happy.

Brittany: I didn't like it either. I always missed one or the other. A lot of times, I cried for the one I wasn't with.

Lauren: I wanted to make sure they were doing okay, and I didn't feel like I could do that when we were at separate houses. It affected my sense of what "home" should feel like.

What were vacations like for you during the divorced years?

Brittany: One thing I remember most about vacations was the airport. I remember thinking that I wanted to tell people around me that my parents were not mean to each other even though they were divorced. I wanted to make sure people knew that they were nice to each other and that our family was okay. I don't understand why I felt the need to tell people that.

Lauren: Of course I have many great memories from vacations, but I hated only having one parent there. It just didn't feel right—it felt unbalanced. I would always want the other parent to come, especially if we were having a lot of fun. I dreaded the fact that one parent would be left home alone for a long period of time. I would cry almost every time we left for a vacation.

What changed in your lives when your parents got back together?

Lauren: I felt wholeness and peace. I felt settled. It was incredible, and it actually took some adjustment because the majority of my life I had not known what it was like to have my parents together in the same house. I felt so blessed watching the love between my parents.

Brittany: I felt a peace that I had never felt before because our family was whole. I was blessed to see Jesus unify our family and mend many of the broken pieces in each of us. I felt I'd actually witnessed something real the Lord had accomplished in our lives. I'm extremely grateful for that now.

What lasting effect has your parents divorce and reconciliation had on you?

Brittany: In some situations, I've struggled with the feeling of abandonment. I don't know if this relates to the divorce, but I believe it does in some situations. I'm really grateful for the blessings that the Lord has given my family in restoration. I feel extremely blessed to have such a beautiful story of reconciliation in my family. I have seen the work the Lord has done, not only in me personally and in my family, but also in the many lives Jesus has transformed through His work of restoration through my parents. I understand more fully the reality of marriage today, and the importance of placing Christ first in every part of our lives. I don't know who I would be today without Christ's powerful work of reconciliation in my family.

Lauren: It has shown me that the grace of God is so powerful, that he always has a plan. I have seen what a marriage is like before and after Jesus. I feel like I am more aware of the reality of marriage—that it's not a fairy tale but simply a reality. Marriage can be a daily struggle. It has also shown me that the things of the world are unfulfilling (my parents' first marriage), that communication is pertinent to having a healthy marriage, and that love must be fought for. I've learned that anyone can be tempted into adultery of many kinds, no matter how strong you think you are.

How do your parents' lives and ministry affect you now?

Lauren: Their lives and ministry have taught me so much. I have never seen someone stand as strong as my mom, and I have never seen anyone as willing to be molded as my dad. Their lives truly show me a beautiful picture of Jesus. My parents speak a lot about the Lord, but what has impacted me the most is watching their lives. They are so dedicated to Jesus, even when times seem impossible and hopeless. Their ministry has taught me a lot about the reality of marriage—how precious it is, how hard it is, how it will rarely work without Jesus as the center. I have seen how authenticity and vulnerability will create ministry and change. I have learned that the purpose of marriage is not to make you happy, but holy. It is primarily about focusing on you and your relationship with Jesus instead of focusing on what the other person is doing wrong. It has shown me the importance of true fellowship with other believers in order to sharpen your marriage and life.

The main thing I've learned is that living with other believers has to be very intentional. Having couples over for dinner and hearing their stories has taught me a ton and I learn so much from their openness about the struggles in their marriages. Instead of trying to hide embarrassing sin, my parents have shared it and that honesty produces greater freedom than trying to keep up a clean image. It has provided a great contrast between the sinful motivations of our hearts and the grace Jesus pours out to heal and restore. And in that way, I see their ministry as a picture of the cross.

Brittany: The reconciliation and ministry that my parents have now has completely transformed my life. I see hundreds of people affected by their story of true life change. I have also been taught what it means to minister and serve other people and the importance of developing true community through meaningful relationships. I have seen the difference this makes in following Jesus Christ and being truly committed to him. The love that Christ has shown us, they show to other people, and I am truly blessed to be a part of that in a family. I have seen real, authentic conversation and honesty, and I would not be the same person I am today without their example of restoration.

A Conversation with Jeff and Cheryl

Since we work in marriage ministry and frequently speak to churches, retreats, and other large groups, we get a lot of questions from people wanting to know more or go deeper into our story. We're happy to share as much as we can if it helps people gain insight into their own relationships and understand what God desires for them.

Of course, we're not theologians or seminarians or pastors. We're everyday Christians giving a testimony of our own experiences and God's work in our lives. For questions of a deeper theological nature, we encourage you to consult with a pastor or other expert. We are simply sharing our experience as honestly as we can.

Here are a few typical questions people ask us, and some brief answers.

What if God isn't going to restore my marriage? How will I know?

In our experience, when people are genuinely seeking God and his will for their lives, they sense his direction. They feel a sense of peace when pursuing his will, and an unexplainable hindrance when going in opposition to his will. Part of seeking God means studying Scripture to see what answers can be gleaned from the Word he's already given us; another aspect of seeking God is obtaining advice from godly people. Between prayer, Scripture, and seeking godly counsel, people can usually get a good handle on what God is speaking into their lives. We typically advise people who doubt the possibility of restoration to work closely with a trusted pastor or

Christian counselor and to pray for discernment so that they don't mistake their own desires for God's voice.

Everyone communicates with God differently, and we all have different words to describe it. You may sense God's direction as a nudge on your conscience or a strong conviction of "the right thing to do." Some people find answers directly from Scripture, and for others, God "speaks" to them through the voice of a trusted friend or mentor. The important thing is to trust that God *does* have a way of communicating his will to you and trust that God has given you your own unique way of hearing him.

Seven years seems like a long time for Cheryl to persist when there was no evidence that Jeff would ever come around. Why did you keep going?

There were many times I (Cheryl) could have turned back. I could have given up. But I kept getting confirmation one way or another that I needed to persevere. Each time, I either came across a line of Scripture that spelled it out for me or had a strong conviction or talked to someone who encouraged me. The affirmations kept coming. And in the times when I wasn't sure, I occasionally gave up, but I kept my heart open to God. He always straightened me out somehow.

If I'd been praying every day and reading Scripture and working at being devoted to the Lord and he never gave me a confirmation that I should pursue Jeff, I suppose it could have gone the other way. I think the main thing is, if there is any confusion or doubt as to what you should do, to err on the side of trusting that God can do the impossible. Keep pursuing restoration. If you feel led *out* of the marriage, it's most likely your desire speaking, not God's. In our experience, God may lead you to separate physically, especially in cases of abuse, addiction, or unrepentant adultery, but it's rare that he will lead you directly to divorce until all options have truly been tried.

You've said that if we feel unhappy in our marriage, we need to take the focus off the relationship and look at ourselves first. Exactly what do you mean by that?

Looking at yourself can take many forms. It helps to start with a type of journaling where you write down your feelings and frustrations and begin to identify possible causes for these feelings. You can do this on your own, but it's usually most effective when done with a counselor, a life coach, or a trusted friend or confidant.

For example, when Cheryl began to feel lonely and discontented early in the first marriage, some honest self-examination probably would have revealed that Jeff wasn't the only source of her frustration. She was frustrated with her lack of close female friends with whom to bond, talk, and spend time. She might have realized that her expectations of the marriage fulfilling all her needs were unrealistic, and she could have started to figure out what else she needed in her life to discover meaning and purpose. An honest exploration could have helped her discover her spiritual emptiness and led her to Jesus. She would have realized that shallowness in the marriage was only a small part of the problem; in fact, it was just a symptom of a larger problem—two people living without a purpose larger than themselves.

To begin repairing a marriage, it's vital to start with where you are, get the help you need, and begin to honestly evaluate your life and your relationship with the Lord.

Since there is biblical grounds for divorce if my spouse has been unfaithful, do I still need to pursue reconciliation?

This is a big question. The majority of people are so wounded by the betrayal that they can't imagine moving past the pain enough to allow for restoration. The hurt can be profound, and we're not trying to minimize that. Jeff knows from experience how the pain of infidelity can radically alter who you are and how you look at life.

However, God can do immeasurably more than you could ever ask or imagine. He can heal your heart, and he can resurrect your marriage, no matter what state it's in.

As mere humans, we tend to limit God, especially in this extreme type of situation. But where there is room for repentance, there is also room for forgiveness and grace. If you can't imagine such a miracle in your situation, choose to believe that God can and does. And in practicing that power you possess to believe God and take him at his word, you will find the strength to commit to acting on that belief. As we know from experience, reconciliation is a matter of trust, and it begins between you and God.

We didn't have to remarry; biblically, the grounds for divorce were sound. But that doesn't negate the truth that God created marriage to be the foundation of the family, and he created the family to be the foundation of society. The best thing we can do for ourselves, our children, and our society as a whole is to preserve marriages. If you choose to give up your right to your ego and your pain and walk the road of forgiveness and grace, you are glorifying God and living according to his purpose. You are giving an immense gift to yourself, your spouse, and your children. If you allow God to heal your heart and bolster you with his grace and love, choosing to walk the difficult path, you will never regret it.

Jeff, how *did* you finally decide to forgive Cheryl?

I knew I needed to forgive Cheryl, but I had a hard time getting to that place. I felt as though I was the victim in the whole thing. But, as I taught the high school guys' Bible study each week, and spent more time in the Word, I realized that I had some personal responsibility for the failure of our marriage. It was not just Cheryl's fault! Once I understood my part in why our marriage failed, I was then able to have compassion for Cheryl's sin and see her as Jesus saw her; a child of his who needed forgiveness.

You don't have to forgive because they deserve it. Frankly, they don't. But just as Jesus chose to forgive us even before we'd repented, the choice to forgive opens the way for the most meaningful growth we can experience in life. If you think you can't possibly forgive, do it instead to set yourself free from that pain. Do it in hopes that trust will one day return. But do it soon, and accept that it's simply a part of living life.

Cheryl, what about the man with whom you had the affair? He's a person too. Doesn't your testimony seem to demean or devalue him?

One of the reasons affairs are so destructive is that so many lives are affected. In this book, we've told you how my actions affected me, Jeff, and our daughters. But others were affected, too, and Todd was one of them. A consequence of my sin was that this man's life was turned upside down. I let him persist for years thinking that his future was with me, so ending the relationship was incredibly hard on him. I've had to ask God's forgiveness for this and hand my remorse over to the Lord. It was difficult to avoid carrying guilt about it because I couldn't do anything to fix it, and I never knew how his life unfolded after we parted. He could have recovered quickly and moved on to marry someone else; or he could have remained devastated for months or even years. I'll never know. I prayed that the consequences of my sin would be erased from his life and that he found some measure of peace. Of course, I prayed that he found the Lord as well. All this is to say that I've never tried to devalue him as a person and a child of God; I simply had to give up *my* right to him, and place him in God's hands.

My marriage has been miserable for years. We've been in and out of counseling, and my spouse always promises to change, but he never does. It's pretty clear he is never going to be the other half of a healthy marriage. What should I do?

This is one of the biggest dilemmas we face on an ongoing basis as we counsel couples. We see marriages where one spouse is verbally or physically abusive, an alcoholic or drug addict, a repeated philanderer without intent to change, or has a mental disorder that is not adequately treated.

The first thing we look at is the safety of the family. If the offending spouse is a danger to the family, we don't recommend staying in the same home with that person, and we insist that qualified help is brought into the picture—a psychologist, pastor, or other professional. Common sense dictates that you protect yourself and your children from someone who may harm you.

Still, even with all the extreme cases we've counseled, we've never suggested divorce. Occasionally we'll recommend separation, especially in abusive situations. But we stress that it isn't a ticket to start dating or a ticket to get on with life. Separation can be a good thing when used for the right purpose—to seriously attempt to get your lives right with God and determine God's will for the purpose of your marriage.

We want people to be healed, and we want marriages to be healed. That's what we pray for all the time. But we don't know God's plans for every couple. Our experience has taught us that God can redeem anything, so we never give up on anyone. But regardless of which direction they go, we let them know that we love them and support them and that God loves them no matter what. If you are in this circumstance, we'd advise you to keep yourself and your children safe, diligently seek the Lord through prayer and Scripture study, obtain godly counsel, and do your best to follow God's leading based on your understanding of him. Never forget that

God loves you, and he will never withhold his love even if you make a mistake.

Cheryl and Jeff, your story was built on a huge crisis—an affair and a divorce. Some people aren't in crisis; they're just unhappy, and they don't know how to fix it. Is it possible to have this paradigm shift without having a crisis?

To be honest, among the couples we work with, the ones who seem to experience profound change are the ones who've recognized their crisis, brought it out in the open, and dealt with it. The reality is that if there is discontent in the marriage, there is a crisis whether you realize it or not. It's easy to ignore it when it's not causing your life to explode. The key is to stop ignoring it.

Cheryl didn't want to "rock the boat" of our marriage when she started to feel frustrated and unhappy, so the problem festered into a huge crisis. What we learned from that is, *don't be afraid to rock the boat.* Don't be afraid to bring a crisis out in the open. It's the only way you can begin to fix it.

However, we realize that many people hearing our testimony or reading this book are not in a crisis. Instead they have some minor issues in their marriage that they need to fix before the issues grow into huge problems. These people can learn, not from their own crisis, but from watching someone else's (in this case, ours). Even in our family, our siblings, our parents, and our daughters have all watched us go through our years of trauma and had their lives changed by it.

In dealing with a situation when it's not (yet) a crisis, a level of selflessness is necessary. Your self-interest might make you want to keep quiet; after all, bringing an issue out in the open means you're going to have to deal with it. You might not feel like you're up for all that drama and possibly trauma. But this is the time to think outside yourself. Is it best for your spouse if you're open rather than withholding? Is it best for your kids if you attempt to improve your marriage before it's too late? Is your whole marriage going to explode if you refuse to address the issues? Like we talked about earlier in the book, some of it is pure self-discipline, getting outside yourself, and admitting what's best for all.

If either partner is frustrated and unhappy, or addicted to anything, including pornography, then there is definitely a crisis, regardless of how picture perfect everything looks from the outside. Don't be afraid to get your crisis out in the open. It's the first step.

Do you promise people that if they obey God and keep their marriage together, God will bless their efforts?

That message comes through in our testimony, but we don't say it outright, and we don't promise it. It's obvious to others that our lives have been blessed, but God doesn't promise that. We have no idea what God is going to do.

We believe that obedience brings peace in your relationship with the Lord. But is there going to be peace in all your other relationships? Not necessarily. Are there going to be tangible "rewards" for obedience? Sometimes it seems God works that way, and sometimes it doesn't. We don't believe God would have rained punishments down on our heads if we'd chosen a different path, since we believe in grace and forgiveness, but we believe if we hadn't reconciled in obedience to what seemed like clear godly direction, we would have missed out on some of the most profound blessings in life.

We are storing up our riches in heaven; he doesn't promise riches here on earth. Even if obedience is directly rewarded with blessing, we have no idea what that blessing looks like. It can be different for everyone.

EPILOGUE

Contentment in marriage can be a matter of perception. Often dissatisfaction sets in because we hold vastly unrealistic expectations—both of marriage and of life. Our culture encourages us to believe that happiness is our birthright and that if we don't have it, something is terribly wrong.

One of the things we've tried to do in our family is expose ourselves to other cultures and other ways of looking at things in order to give our lives some perspective. The daily life of the average American is so incredibly pampered and luxurious compared to most of the world. The things we perceive as a lack of "fulfillment" would be viewed by ninety percent of the earth's population as needless whining and idealistic beliefs. We've found that when people take the focus off themselves and begin serving others, it can impart profound lessons and facilitate paradigm shifts about every aspect of our lives, including marriage. Here is one of the ways it happened for our family.

Jeff

We went on a mission trip to Cuba—Cheryl, Lauren, Brittany, and I. The girls were teenagers at the time. Our family was put into a group with an interpreter and a local evangelical Christian pastor, so there were six of us traveling together. We met during the daytime at a church to minister to local Cuban pastors who came from miles around to spend time with us.

They hitchhiked, walked—whatever they had to do. Some had traveled for fifteen hours or more.

All the pastors stayed in one house, while our group stayed in a luxury hotel. At least, it was luxurious by their standards, but it wasn't a luxury hotel by our standards! We'd get back to our room each night at ten thirty or eleven and complain to each other, "I'm so exhausted." We'd say a two-minute prayer and go to sleep. In the morning we'd get up, have breakfast, and drive out to meet the pastors again.

On the second day, all the pastors looked really tired, so we asked them if they were okay. We didn't know what was wrong.

It turned out they'd stayed up until five in the morning, just praying for what we were going to do that day! That impacted us deeply. We're supposed to be on this mission trip to serve God's people, and we were complaining when we got back to the hotel at night that we were so tired, the bed was kind of lumpy, and the pillows weren't what we were used to. These guys were lying on mats that weren't even a good quality sleeping bag by our standards and staying up all night praying. It put things in perspective.

One day we had to go by our interpreter's house because he had forgotten his medicine. He lived in a concrete building maybe as big as our hotel room. His closet, which was the size of a small table, contained one other shirt, one other pair of pants, and one other pair of shoes, and that was it. It was incredible for our daughters to see that. None of us could imagine owning only two outfits. Our interpreter also had a huge pig in his yard. Lauren has always loved pigs; she was enthralled with his "pet pig" and told him so. He sort of raised his eyebrows and grinned at her. "Pet pig? What do you mean? That's Christmas dinner!"

We live so differently from most of the world, and we think differently. How we live and think gives us our perspective. Most people, whose daily preoccupation is something more basic, like survival or spreading the gospel, can't fathom our obsession with happiness and contentment all the time.

The idea of perspective is so important. What is your perspective?

What we wanted to do with this book was offer hope for marriages through a paradigm shift. It comes from taking a different perspective— getting your eyes off yourself and putting them on the Lord.

We have a passionate desire to see marriages changed, made whole, and restored. Our prayer is that more and more marriages will epitomize God's plan, not society's. Although the world seems to hold virtually no hope for marriages and families being restored, we want to spread the word that "by his mighty power at work within us, he is able to accomplish infinitely more than we would ever dare to ask or hope" (Ephesians 3:20, NLT). It is possible for a marriage to be made brand-new!

If you can trust God to show you the bigger picture of your marriage, *he will do it.* Proverbs 3:5–6 says, "Trust in the LORD with all your heart and lean not on your own understanding; in all your ways acknowledge him, and he will make your paths straight." In other words, he will direct you and make it clear where you are to go.

One more question people ask us is "How is your marriage today?" We were married for ten years in a self-focused, worldly relationship without Christ. Now (at this writing) we've been married eight years in a wonderful, Christ-centered union. The funny thing is that people think we must have a perfect marriage. (But people thought that about our first marriage too.) Of course, it's not true. We have struggles, disagreements, and bad days like everyone else. The difference is our undying commitment to each other. There is never any doubt that both of us are in the marriage "till death." Even though eight years have passed, we still start each day grateful for all that happened. We realize it's rare to get a second chance at this thing. We'll never take it for granted, ever. We do our best to live every day to serve and glorify God, serving *each other* for God. It is the foundation of how we function.

We're now becoming partial empty nesters, and some people are concerned about what will happen to our marriage when the kids leave home. To tell the truth, in our first marriage, I worried about this too. But honestly, we never worry about the kids leaving home because of how strongly we know that our marriage is restored and our family mended. Our marriage is better now than ever before. We sometimes act and feel like newlyweds, and the intimacy continues to go deeper. It is definitely a challenge to get used to our kids going their own way, but we see it as a new, exciting season of life.

Our lives are so full of meaning and purpose. Our marriage itself has a much bigger purpose than "Jeff and Cheryl being married to each other." We endeavor to live out God's purpose for marriage, amidst the joys, the trials, the challenges, and the overpowering love. This "marriage thing" is a journey that is sometimes easy and sometimes tough. But because of our unique experience, we have become more purposeful in helping others see a different, deeper side of marriage, one that is richer and more fulfilling than most people imagine. We are blessed to be able to pour into others and share our story in hopes that God can redeem whatever trial others are going through in their marriages. What gives our lives purpose is living for God, not living for ourselves.

We encourage you not to lose hope…to place your trust in God…to hang in there and not give up. God miraculously gave us our family back, and we pray the same for you. Above all else, we give God the glory!

RESOURCES

BOOK RECOMMENDATIONS

Marriage
Sacred Marriage by Gary L. Thomas
The Book of Romance by Tommy Nelson
How We Love by Milan and Kay Yerkovich
Sacred Sex: A Spiritual Celebration of Oneness in Marriage by Tim
    Alan Gardner and Scott M. Stanley
The Mystery of Marriage by Mike Mason
How to Save Your Marriage Alone by Ed Wheat
Marriage on the Rock by Jimmy Evans
Intimate Issues by Linda Dillow and Lorraine Pintus
Love & Respect by Emerson Eggerichs
War of Words by Paul David Tripp
Connecting by Larry Crabb
Age of Opportunity by Paul David Tripp

General Christianity
In a Pit with a Lion on a Snowy Day by Mark Batterson
When People Are Big and God Is Small by Edward T. Welch
Knowing God by J. I. Packer
Celebration of Discipline by Richard J. Foster
Shattered Dreams by Larry Crabb

Don't Waste Your Life by John Piper
Desiring God by John Piper
Soul Talk by Larry Crabb
Total Forgiveness by R.T. Kendall

Affairs and Addictions

Surviving an Affair by Willard F. Harley Jr. and Jennifer Harley
    Chalmers
Avoiding the Greener Grass Syndrome by Nancy C. Anderson
Torn Asunder: Recovering from an Extramarital Affair by Dave
    Carder
False Intimacy: Understanding the Struggle of Sexual Addiction
    by Dr. Harry W. Schaumburg

Separation and Divorce

When Love Dies by Judy Bodmer

For Men

Point Man by Steve Farrar
The Silence of Adam by Larry Crabb
Finishing Strong by Steve Farrar

For Women

Words of Wisdom for Women at the Well by Shannon Ethridge
Choices by Mary Farrar
Sacred Influence by Gary L. Thomas
Reading Your Male by Mary Farrar (releasing February 2009)

INTERNET RESOURCES

Hope Matters Marriage Ministries, Inc.

www.hopeformarriages.com

www.hopemattersmarriage.blogspot.com

The Village Church—Matt Chandler

www.thevillagechurch.net

Matt Chandler's podcast: www.thevillagechurch.net/podcast

The Center for Evangelical Spirituality

www.garythomas.com

Steve Farrar

http://stevefarrar.com/

Song of Solomon Bible Resources

www.songofsolomon.com

ACKNOWLEDGMENTS

Many years ago when I (Cheryl) first sat down to start taking notes for this book, I was clueless about the circuitous route it would take to publication. I was especially ignorant about the number of people that would have to get on board for it to happen. It has only become a reality thanks to the faithful support, prayers, and practical help of an astounding group of friends and publishing professionals.

First we want to express our thanks to God for the journey that is chronicled in this book, and for his grace in allowing us to share it with others. We pray God will work through these words to bring about miracles in many other marriages.

Our deepest thanks to the staff at WaterBrook Press, especially Mick Silva, for believing in this project and grasping the vision for it. Thanks, Mick, for your insightful and sensitive editorial guidance.

To Greg Johnson, our agent. We could not have done it without you! Thank you for sticking your neck out and believing in a couple of unknown writers.

To Rachelle Gardner, an incredible wordsmith. You made the book come alive! Thank you for your patience and gentle spirit when we had no idea what we were doing.

To Gary Thomas, thank you for your God-breathed words in *Sacred Marriage*. It took us to a new level of understanding God's plan for a biblical marriage, and is providing us a resource with which to teach couples.

To Steve and Mary Farrar, your deep friendship means so much, and we could not have come this far without your guidance in countless ways.

To Karol Ladd, thank you for encouraging Cheryl early on and showing her the ropes when she had no idea where to start in the process of writing and publishing a book.

To Pete Briscoe, Senior Pastor at Bent Tree Bible Church. Your boldness in encouraging us to share our story publicly has made all the difference. You reminded us that God gave us our story for a reason, to share it to the ends of the earth for the glory of God. Thank you.

To Matt Chandler, our lead pastor at The Village Church. We cannot express in words how grateful we are for your authenticity and genuine, transparent heart which shows through in your personal life and from the pulpit. Thank you for boldly sharing God's word without apology!

To our parents, Dick and Shirley Kies, and Thurman and Peggy Scruggs, thank you for your dedication to us and to each other in marriage. It is an awesome blessing to see your commitment remain strong through thick and thin for over fifty years. You gave us incredible examples to live up to, and we are so grateful.

To Cheryl's friends—Donna, Melanie and Steve, Rosie, and Paulette—for allowing me to cry on your shoulders for seven years while waiting on the miracle.

To friends and family who have encouraged us, prayed for us, and been our cheerleaders along the way: Sharon Kendall, Dan Garrison, Chris Wilson, Cynthia Jehl, Dan and Susan Chapman, Chris and Dana Crawford, and countless more. Also to Erika Palmacci, a fifth grader who was bold enough to speak truth into Jeff's life about why God wanted us to reconcile. Thank you all for believing that God's miracle of reconciliation in our lives could be used by God to encourage others.

To our board members at Hope Matters Marriage Ministries for their belief in what we have been called forward to do and for their support in so many ways.

To all of our incredible friends, too many to mention by name. We love you and thank you for your support, encouragement, prayers, love and believing in the hope for whole and healed marriages.

To the hundreds of couples that have come across our path. We thank God for you and pray that the Lord would work in your marriage as he has in ours.

From Cheryl… to my husband, Jeff. Thank you for your understanding, your patience, your forgiveness and your support far beyond what I could have ever asked or dreamed. Thank you for believing in me, even after all we have been through.

From Jeff… to my wife, Cheryl, who by humble submission to Jesus saw the vision for a renewed and restored marriage for us and our family. Thanks for listening to God and walking in his ways.

Finally and most importantly, to our beautiful girls, Brittany and Lauren. Thank you for your undying patience and endurance during the tough years, for persevering in daily prayer for the reconciliation, and for believing in God for the miracle. Thank you for your forgiveness and love—it is beyond comprehension at times. Thank you for allowing us to share your story along with ours, and for contributing your words. You will always be our biggest inspiration.

ABOUT JEFF AND CHERYL

J eff and Cheryl Scruggs are the founders of Hope Matters Marriage Ministries, Inc. which exists to share their passion to see marriages changed, made whole, and reconciled to God's plan. Claiming the promise that "by his mighty power at work within us, he is able to accomplish infinitely more than we would ever dare to ask or hope" (Ephesians 3:20, NLT), Jeff and Cheryl have seen countless marriages made new again. They offer marriage counseling through their ministry, and Cheryl is also on staff at the Center for Christian Counseling in Flower Mound and Frisco, Texas.

Jeff and Cheryl live in the Dallas area, and have two grown daughters who currently attend college.